THANK YOU FOR FINDING this BOOK to KEEP OR SHARE. WE HOPE that SOME OF ERIN's will touch you and INSPIRE YOU IN YOUR life's JOURNEY. PLEASE SHARE HER messages with others around you. The WORLD NEEDS a DOSE OF HOPE. WE WISH YOU well.

LOVE FROM ERIN's PARENTS ~
Kathy and Abel

THE LOUDEST QUIET GIRL: MESSAGES OF HOPE IN A DARK WORLD

THE SHORT FULL LIFE AND INSPIRATIONAL WRITINGS OF ERIN KATE RODRIQUES

KATHY RODRIQUES

Kathy Rodriques

authorHOUSE®

AuthorHouse™
1663 Liberty Drive
Bloomington, IN 47403
www.authorhouse.com
Phone: 1 (800) 839-8640

Unless otherwise noted, photos are provided by the author; all photos are used with permission of models and photographers.

The poem "Footprints" is reprinted by permission of the author, Carolyn Joyce Carty.

Excerpt from The Lord of the Rings by J. R. R. Tolkien, edited by Christopher Tolkien. Copyright 1954, 1955, 1965, 1966 by J. R. R. Tolkien. Copyright renewed 1982, 1983 by Christopher R. Tolkien, Michael H. R. Tolkien, John F. R. Tolkien, and Priscilla M. A. R. Tolkien. Copyright renewed 1993, 1994 by Christopher R. Tolkien, John F. R. Tolkien, and Priscilla M. A. R. Tolkien. Reprinted by permission of Houghton Mifflin Harcourt Publishing Company. All rights reserved.

Published by AuthorHouse 11/27/2019

Front cover photo of Erin by Anna Gorin, used with permission.

Back cover photo is provided by the author and used with permission of the model.

ISBN: 978-1-7283-2370-1 (sc)
ISBN: 978-1-7283-2369-5 (hc)
ISBN: 978-1-7283-2371-8 (e)

Library of Congress Control Number: 2019912038

Print information available on the last page.

This book is printed on acid-free paper.

CONTENTS

PART 1

THE END OF LIFE AS WE KNEW IT

❖

PART 2

ERIN'S EARLY YEARS

❖

PART 3

MIDDLE YEARS

❖

PART 4

YOUR ADULT YEARS

◆

PART 5

FROM ERIN'S PHYSICAL DEATH TO HER NEW LIFE

◆

PART 6

AFTERWORD

◆

FOREWORD

Every once in a while we are fortunate to come to know individuals who leave a lasting impression on our lives. Erin Rodriques was such a person. I came to know Erin on a pilgrimage sponsored by Assumption College to France and Rome several years ago. While she was still an undergraduate at the time, I noticed several qualities about Erin that pointed to someone mature beyond her years. On the surface, she was quiet, one might say shy, that in reality revealed her reflective and contemplative nature, marveling in everything around her. When she spoke, she was soft spoken, highlighting a gentleness and humility that manifested her awareness of the grandeur of God's creation, of which she knew she was one small, yet important, part. Erin possessed a depth of soul that was nurtured by her Catholic faith that grounded her life and all that she did both great and small.

Erin was an avid photographer, which I witnessed on our pilgrimage. Wherever we went, her camera was with her. What I noticed, though, was that she wasn't simply taking photos of typical tourist sites of significance, but of ordinary things that one would not even notice. But, Erin noticed, whether it was a flower, a squirrel or a bird, elderly men playing cards, young couples sitting on a park bench holding hands, a storefront or decorative window display, children walking home from school, as well as scenes of nature from sunsets to clouds gliding across the sky. She noticed these aspects of life because she reveled in the ordinariness of life, which for her was extraordinary. What made life extraordinary for Erin was its beauty. She recognized the beauty of the world because she saw the face of God in everything around her. Indeed, she was enamored with the beauty of the world which for her was a manifestation of God's love that filled her soul, her life, and her spirit.

Erin herself reflected this beauty, which she brought to the world. She possessed an inner beauty which shone through her eyes, her smile and her gentle spirit.

This collection of Erin's writings speak to an abiding love that Erin had for God—a love that gave her strength and made her special. God's love gave meaning to all she did. Erin touched many people each and every day because she reflected the image of God's love in simple, ordinary ways. In this way, she was extraordinary. While she is missed by her parents, fiancé, family and friends she remains with us in our memories, in our hearts, and in these words that will speak to each reader in their own unique way. Erin has left us messages of hope that remind us of the relationship she had with God in this life and now has more abundantly as she dwells in the presence of the One whom she loved, "the Love," as Dante writes in the last canto of the *Paradiso* in *The Divine Comedy*, "that moves the sun and the other stars" (*Paradiso* XXXIII, 145).

Francesco C. Cesareo, PhD
President
Assumption College

ACKNOWLEDGMENTS

Thanks to God for the gift of Erin, who brought so much joy, life, and love into our lives. Thanks to our beautiful Erin for leaving us these insights into her inner life and knowing she would want us to share them. Thanks to Josh, Erin's fiancé, who found and gave to us her journals from high school, not knowing what a comforting and inspirational gift they would be. Thanks to my husband, Abel, Erin's father, who helped me remember long-filed-away events in our lives and gave me the quiet space to complete this project.

Much appreciation to Monsignor John McLaughlin for allowing me to use his reference to Erin in her funeral homily as "the loudest quiet girl"[1] for the title of this book. In addition, thanks to Patrick Logan for his permission,[2] as he coined the term originally (to the best of our knowledge).

Also, gratitude to those who nagged—I mean encouraged!—me to follow through with sharing Erin's life and writings with the world, especially to our families and friends; Barry Walsh, our therapist; Cindy Washbourne, Erin's work colleague and now our friend; Patricia Johnston, a prayerful and insightful family friend; and Dr. Gail Tsimprea, both a family friend and McLean colleague. Also thanks for the encouragement and support from my fellow Northeastern University classmates Linda Bertolami (and her husband, Charles); Anne and Steve Ottariano; Chris and Gene Johnson; and Maryann and Andy Chiras, who sent me every Christmas newsletter we had sent to them through the years. I am grateful to those who reviewed and critiqued the manuscript, especially Dawn Fletcher, our massage therapist and friend, an avid reader who helped me with meaningful content ideas; Jane McDonald and her husband, Arthur Siegel, my friends and work colleagues from McLean Hospital, also avid readers who knew Erin since before she was born and reminded us of forgotten events that were essential to the book; and Barry Walsh, again, for his suggestions as an author himself. Great thanks to Deacon Paul Kline and his wife, Rosemary, our friends, for their insightful reviews[3] and suggestions on the content of the book. Thanks to all of our family and friends who have been praying us through this rough time in our lives. We appreciate it so much.

Grateful thanks to the faculty and staff of Assumption College in Worcester, Massachusetts, who helped bolster our faith, continued their comfort during the years following the accident, and invited us to have a beautiful memorial garden for Erin on their campus. A big thank-you to Anna Gorin, Erin's (and now our) friend, for her photographic assistance and many gorgeous photos from shoots she did with Erin. Additionally, thanks to Abel's brother Dean, who came to my rescue when my laptop got entangled in a tech-support scam. He professionally rescanned all Erin's journal pages and photos. What a weight off my shoulders!

Special thanks to Francesco Cesareo, president of Assumption College, for writing the foreword and sharing his special thoughts of Erin, whom he came to know and love. His clear analysis of Erin lovingly and accurately summarizes her personality and soul.[4]

Thanks to Erin's many friends who shared stories with us of their unique relationships with Erin. I am grateful to too many people to name, but you know who you are. I apologize if I have left anyone out. Thanks for being friends to Erin and to us in this game of life. May you feel Erin's presence, especially on your dark days. May her life be a beacon of light for you.

INTRODUCTION

December 9 will forever hold a pall of darkness over us, as that is the day our beautiful only child, Erin, died tragically at the age of twenty-three, five months before her upcoming marriage. It holds sadness not only for us, her parents, but also for her fiancé and his family, her grandmothers, and her many family members and friends. Even acquaintances mourned for her.

A few months after Erin died, her fiancé, Josh, gave us some of her journals that he had come across. She had begun writing them around early high school age. I had known she kept journals, but I never had looked at them. I was surprised to see how deep her writings were at such a young age. Whether intentionally or not, they were filled with personal and inspirational messages for those she left behind—messages filled with *hope*. Since my first reading of these entries, I have felt the need to share them with as many people as I can because the world can be such a dark place. I know she would want to share her writings freely, as many of them were written in a way that seemed to address the reader. I have extracted the more inspirational entries and interspersed them throughout the book. At the end of this introduction, I have included the entry I was most comforted by, which placed in me the burning need to share her writings with others. Erin wrote this particular entry on May 26, 2006, when she was fifteen years old. Following Erin's journal entry, I have included the "Footprints" prayer so you can read it more easily. Incidentally, that was the prayer we used on the back of Erin's memorial cards at the time of her funeral—three months before we found this journal entry.

There are many more entries, but most of the others pertain to the usual everyday dramas and comedies of life.

We shared Erin's writings with a friend of ours, Deacon Paul Kline. He said I mentioned that I was struck "by how often she seemed to be speaking directly to someone she would never even know at some point in the future." He remarked, "I think this is a very powerful feature of her writings." In his experience, he told me, "teens and young adults usually journal in ways that reflect an *inward* vision—writing about how they see their personal experience and inner world of wishes, fears, frustrations, and wonderings. Erin's writings are unusual, as you say, because they so often reflect the experiences of someone who is looking *outside* and speaking to others in a way that responds to what someone else might be feeling. This uncanny and intuitive empathy is one of the most cherished gifts Erin offers the reader."[5]

Even though my desire to share these messages was strong, it has taken more than four years for my brain, heart, and emotions to pull it all together. My aim was merely to disseminate her messages, but the publisher suggested I add Erin's biography to the book so readers are able to learn more about Erin's life and perhaps have some insight into the reasons she wrote what she did. Through this publication, I hope to continue Erin's legacy and inspire others to follow her path.

I tried to remember Erin's life events the best I could with the help of my husband, Abel. Grieving left us with some memory loss and brain fog, which I already had from past chemo and radiation, so these are the facts to the best of my knowledge. Of course, I also have a parent's bias of my nearly perfect child! I'm sure some of you will say, "That's not the Erin I knew," but this is the Erin *we* knew. I have added some of the more meaningful and funny episodes of her life, complete with photos, in the hope that you will be able to encounter the real Erin, with her full-of-life personality and warmth. In addition to those, there are quotes from several friends about their relationships with Erin so you can get alternate views.

Erin was beautiful inside and out. She had the gift of listening well to people of all ages. Anyone who met her became her best friend. She was an adviser and comforter to many. She at first seemed quiet to those who didn't know her, but they soon discovered that she had a terrific sense of humor and the ability to raise people up and out of their down moods. Erin had extreme compassion and empathy for people. She never judged people and seemed to understand why they did what they did. She called her friends and family and all her animal friends "Lovies" and loved all things purple. Erin had her own anxieties and a little depression, as many of us have, but her strong faith, hope, and love, as can be seen in her writings, managed to pull her through those rough patches. I'd like to share those writings with you in the hope that her advice will gently guide you through your own life's valleys and hills.

Kathy Rodriques (with Abel's assistance)
May 12, 2019, Mother's Day

So even though there have been a few bumps in the road, life is good. But I know that it would never be unless I had trusted God and put my life into His hands. I hope that whoever may be reading this in the future, if you are going through a hard time or do in the future, please, NEVER lose hope! God is always there for you and He will never leave your side. I suggest reading "Footprints". Please just place all your worries in His hands and let His Will be done, it will all be good, this I promise you! I will be praying for you. :)

"Footprints"

One night a man had a dream. He dreamed he was walking along the beach with the Lord. Across the sky flashed scenes from his life. For each scene he noticed two sets of footprints in the sand; one belonged to him and the other to the Lord. When the last scene flashed before him, he looked back on the footprints in the sand. He noticed that many times along the path of his life there was only one set of footprints. He also noticed that it happened at the very lowest and saddest times in his life. This really bothered him and he questioned the Lord about it. "Lord, you said that once I decided to follow you, you'd walk with me all the way. But I have noticed that during the most troublesome times in my life, there is only one set of footprints. I don't understand why when I needed you most you would leave me?" The Lord replied, "My precious, precious child, I love you and I would never leave you. During your times of trial and suffering, when you see only one set of footprints, it was then that

I carried you."

May the Lord be with you now and always.

Footprints

One night a man had a dream. He dreamed he was walking along the beach with the Lord. Across the sky flashed scenes from his life. For each scene, he noticed two sets of footprints in the sand; one belonging to him, and the other to the Lord.

When the last scene of his life flashed before him, he looked back at the footprints in the sand. He noticed that many times along the path of his life there was only one set of footprints. He also noticed that it happened at the very lowest and saddest times in his life.

This really bothered him and he questioned the Lord about it. "Lord, you said that once I decided to follow you, you'd walk with me all the way. But I have noticed that during the most troublesome times in my life, there is only one set of footprints. I don't understand why when I needed you most you would leave me."

The Lord replied, "My precious, precious child, I love you and I would never leave you. During your times of trial and suffering, when you see only one set of footprints, it was then that

I carried you."

—Reprinted with permission from Carolyn Joyce Carty[6]

PART 1

THE END OF LIFE AS WE KNEW IT

I hope that whoever may be reading this in the
future, if you are going through a hard time or do in
the future, please *NEVER* lose hope! God is always
there for you and He will never leave your side.
—Erin Rodriques, May 26, 2006 (fifteen years old)

CHAPTER 1

WEEK OF UNIMAGINABLE TRAUMA AND PAIN

Monday, December 9, 2013, a typical icy and sleety New England winter day, became a surreal nightmare for our family and many others. After working all day, my husband, Abel, and I were relaxing in front of the television. Multitasking as usual, while talking to my mother, Grammy, on the phone, I checked my email around nine o'clock. I was surprised to see an email from a work colleague of our daughter, Erin. He was checking to see if we had heard from her that day. He had been supposed to touch base with her after her new job training, and she hadn't answered any of his calls. I then remembered I had called her at lunchtime, and she hadn't picked up. I had assumed she was busy at training and would call me later. A sick feeling hit my stomach. It was unusual for Erin to be out of touch with us or her friends for that long.

After telling my mother the startling news, I hung up the phone and quickly replied to Erin's colleague. Then I called her fiancé, Josh. When Josh answered, the worry in his voice confirmed my sick stomach. He hadn't heard from Erin either. She'd had a couple appointments after her training, but he'd expected her home by eight thirty or so. I told him to call his parents and said I would notify his local police department. Fortunately, I managed to persuade the police dispatcher that it was unlike Erin to be out of touch with her friends and family during the day; I was in contact with her almost daily. Then Abel and I drove to Erin and Josh's house, which was more than an hour away, hoping to determine what was happening.

When we arrived at Josh's around one o'clock in the morning, a policeman was already there. Josh told us the last time he had heard from Erin had been when she left the house around eight thirty that morning to go to the training class. She had been unable to find her phone, so they'd scrambled around looking for it. When they'd found it, she'd put it in her pocket and left. The policeman had searched the premises before we arrived and assured us that the local and surrounding police were looking for Erin's car. Nothing had shown up yet. I kept thinking that she might have gone off the road and couldn't be seen by searchers. The thought kept surfacing in my mind all night that her car had gone into a body of water, as there were many nearby.

By the early morning hours, the police were treating the case as a criminal investigation. The state police had become involved as well, and an air search would begin as soon as the snow allowed the plane to leave. Josh's parents drove around in the dark, looking for her car. Josh paced around the house, clutching Elainna, their beloved adopted cat. He wanted to be there if Erin arrived home.

I was terrified someone had kidnapped her on her way in to work that morning. Sometimes on her way to work, she would stop at a coffee shop that had some people in need standing around, and she was always willing to give them money or a smile. I constantly was reminded of the horrific kidnapping and murder just six weeks before of a beautiful young teacher who had graduated a year ahead of Erin from the same college. Our scenario was similar. Her parents and the police had searched for her overnight before their unimaginable discovery. An attractive and kind woman's life had been senselessly and grotesquely snuffed out. I was imagining the same horrific fate for Erin, another beautiful and kind young woman. We were all sick to death, wondering what was happening with her. Was she being tortured? Was she dead? Was she still alive? These questions clouded my brain, but I was unable to verbalize them.

In the morning, while Josh's father and Abel retraced Erin's probable drive to and from the training, Josh's mother and I sat at the police station, calling the bank and credit card companies, checking to see if her cards had been used anywhere. Nothing.

The search plane was still waiting for the snow to decrease before venturing out. All of a sudden, we heard the police dispatcher call to the staff that Erin's father was on the phone, saying he had found Erin's car upside down, with just the tires barely visible, in a pond on their street. Josh's mother and I flew down the street to find Abel, Josh's father, and Josh distraught at the accident site. Emergency vehicles began to arrive. The caring officer who had been with us all night remained on duty Tuesday morning and escorted Abel and me into an ambulance that was parallel to Erin's car in the pond. They kept us sheltered there during the recovery efforts. Divers went into the pond, thinking they were going to be able to rescue Erin. They didn't realize she had most likely been there since the day before on her way to work. They were devastated that they couldn't save her. It didn't make it any easier that it was two weeks before Christmas and that most of them had young families themselves.

It was surreal, unimaginable, and evil. I called different people to tell them what had happened, because I knew it was already on the news that she was missing—and now found. I didn't want our friends and family to find out that way. My brain could not and still does not recall any of the conversations or texts. My mind was numb, feeling nothing. Our beautiful, loving only child, just twenty-three, was excited about her new job, had just started graduate school for rehabilitation counseling, and was going to marry her love, Josh, in five months. I had picked out my mother-of-the-bride gown only two days before. This couldn't be real! All this horror, and she never even knew the training had been canceled due to the bad weather.

I won't go into the details of the devastating scene, as they are too personal and painful for those who were there. As we found out in the police report ten months later, it appears that most likely, her car skidded down the icy hill around the corner from their house. Marks from both tires on the left side of the car appeared to go alongside the street side of the pond. She might have been steering out of a skid but then hit a rough opening in the ground that caused the car to flip over down into the pond. Her cell phone was found in her pocket, so we know that was not involved. Her seat belt was still on. We have many unanswered questions. Did she swerve to avoid another car or an animal? Did someone run her off the road? Did she pass out? No answers to these would change the outcome, though.

The rest of that week, friends, family, and colleagues poured through our house, trying to comfort and feed us, all trying to understand how this could have happened. Erin had recently been showing them all the photos of her engagement to Josh and of her trying on her wedding gown. How could we be planning her funeral now? We all had been on such a happy path toward the wedding, and then *smack*—right into a brick wall.

Some of Erin's high school Lifeteen friends, family, and neighbors stopped by our house to bring homemade food and help us put the funeral Mass together with meaningful songs and Scripture readings. Her college and lifelong friends joined us in relating warm and humorous memories of Erin. I remember one story that made me smile and laugh. Her college friend Chris remembers driving up to a red light on his way to school. When he turned his head to look at the car next to him, there was Erin with her signature oversized sunglasses on, bouncing around and singing to the music, not caring if anyone was watching or not. We loved it when her free-spirit self took over.

I don't remember what happened most of that week. My mind seemed to go into a shut-down-of-feelings emergency mode to get through everything we were going to have to plan—the trips to the funeral home to pick out a casket, memorial cards, wake and funeral arrangements, and so on. Fortunately, surrounded by family and friends taking care of life's necessities, we survived the next few weeks.

Erin's wake was held the following Monday, a week after the accident. It lasted three hours longer than announced due to the surge of people coming through. Despite the frigid below-zero-wind-chill-factor night, queues of people wound throughout the funeral home; outside, there remained a long line of people waiting to get in, trying to stay warm, and exchanging their Erin memories. They brought beautiful flowers, Mass cards, sympathy cards, and much love for our beautiful girl.

Friends, family, and colleagues packed the church for Erin's funeral. Many drove or flew long distances in the terrible weather. Another freezing day with snow was predicted. Our friend Father Greg Mathias, who had planned to perform Josh and Erin's wedding in May, became instead the main celebrant of Erin's funeral. Monsignor John McLaughlin, her St. Mary's Lifeteen priest during her high school years, gave a beautiful homily that had everyone laughing and crying. Erin was the loudest quiet girl he'd ever known, he said. There were no dry eyes in the congregation or in the sanctuary, where there were about eight priests and brothers who had known Erin from different activities or school. Bernie Choiniere, the music director in her Lifeteen years, sang special songs for her during the Mass, including "Fly like a Bird" by Ken Canedo and "Coming Home" by J. A. Genito, Order of Saint Augustine. Cousins and good friends were the pallbearers. Some carried the casket; others walked behind it. A heartfelt program booklet was created by two of her good friends, Joe and Katie. During the Mass, I had a surreal and comforting feeling that those in the sanctuary, we in the front row, and Erin's casket were enclosed in a safe bubble, as if it were a taste of Heaven. The feeling is hard to describe.

As we left the church, huge snowflakes were falling, bringing to mind the day only a month before when Abel, Erin, and I had left the local shopping mall after meeting there for lunch in the food court. That day, the same type of huge snowflakes had been falling as Erin went off to her car, carrying the wedding gown she had just chosen at the bridal store. Huge snowflakes fell for two different weddings: bride of Josh and now bride of Christ.

I don't remember much from the cemetery, where many came and gathered with us. From there, we went to the reception, where we had on display numerous photo posters of Erin's life and a video of her photos that our friends Joe and Charlie had created—none of which I could look at, but I greatly appreciated them.

Chapter 2

Coping with our Unexpected, Painful Loss

Days moved into weeks, months, and, now, five years of our new existence without our animated daughter. Life was empty. Making phone calls to life insurance companies and her credit card companies, canceling her upcoming appointments, letting others know that our daughter had died, and trying to speak those words without bursting into tears, so they could understand what I was saying, was painful. I changed the ring tone on my cell phone because I jumped every time it went off, thinking it was Erin. She was usually the only person to text or call me. I needed a new sound that didn't connect with her.

I searched for answers. Did God plan this? Did He allow it? Did He have nothing to do with it? Where is Erin now? Did she suffer? Had she been conscious and afraid? I had many questions and few answers, none of which were definite. The words to my daily prayers were lost from my head. I was not in the world anymore. Little by little, through therapy, reading when I could finally focus, the prayers and consolation of friends and family, and Erin's powerful new guidance, my faith grew stronger. It grew stronger than it had been before, but it took several years. I had to walk the talk about the afterlife I claimed to have believed in all those years. The word *hope* continually came to my mind, especially in those first few months. It would just pop into the forefront of my mind unexpectedly, even before we found Erin's journals. Eventually, hope—and trust that there is more life after our physical deaths—settled in.

Abel and I began therapy a couple weeks after her funeral. The director of the program where Erin had worked for her last three months had reached out to us and offered his services. Dr. Barry Walsh guided us through that horrible ordeal for almost four years. He laughed with us, cried with us, grieved that he had never had the chance to meet Erin, and was amazed at the written and digital legacy that such a young person had left behind. Erin lived more experiences in her short twenty-three years than most people will do in ninety. The three of us understood that when you lose a child, there is no closure or sense of "They are gone, and that's it. Put it behind you, and continue on." No. That doesn't work when parents lose children. You need to know they are still with you and are okay. The loneliness and aching pain of missing her will remain with us until we see her again one day.

This trauma, of course, affected not only us but also many others: her fiancé, Josh, especially; his parents and family; and Erin's grandmothers and other family members. I've read that grandparents are often the overlooked bereaved. They have it doubly hard. They've lost their grandchildren and also feel great pain in watching their own children suffering so deeply, and there's nothing they can do to alleviate their pain. Also affected were Erin's teachers, friends (and anyone who knew her was her friend), family, acquaintances, work colleagues, and belly-dancing classmates. Many people were traumatized. Most of them remember the moment they found out that Erin was missing and then learned that she had drowned in the car accident. It was like when someone asked, "Where were you when John Kennedy was assassinated?" or "Where were you when you heard about 9/11?" Those moments were etched in one's brain forever. Now Erin's moment was engraved there as well. The timing of events is now referred to as "before the accident" or "since the accident."

Our new lives consisted of the attitude "Fake it till you make it." It took months before we could even go into a grocery store. Between being triggered by seeing certain foods that Erin would have been buying and trying to avoid people we knew because it would be awkward for them to figure out the right thing to say to us—which was pretty much nothing—it was difficult to go out in public, even to church, and of course, we knew we would burst out crying if anyone said anything nice to us. I burst out crying at one store because a gift card Erin had given us wouldn't work. We eventually found out that the gift card number had been stolen by someone and used in California. Normally, that is not a situation I would have cried about, but Erin's writing was on the gift card, and I felt as if the thief had personally stolen it from her. It was hard to go to the movies, a favorite thing the three of us did together, so we didn't go for a long time. We still cannot watch anything that has a wedding in it. The pain is still too great. There were many grief triggers around us because everywhere we went in town was a place where Erin had spent time, especially the library. To this day, it is still difficult for us to go there. We were always together, the Three Musketeers. It didn't seem right with only the two of us. My heart ached, and still does, for Josh. At least we enjoyed Erin for twenty-three years. He only knew her for three and looked forward to being with her for the rest of his life. It was, and still is, so sad.

Almost a year after the accident, Abel and I participated in a weekend retreat for grieving parents, sponsored by the Emmaus Ministry for Grieving Parents based at St. Anthony's Shrine in downtown Boston. The retreat was held in a town on the South Shore of Boston, not far from the ocean. We were a bit afraid to go because we didn't know what to expect and thought we would be crying all weekend. It turned out to be comforting. Everyone there had lost a child, so we knew the type of different and deep pain we all were experiencing. We didn't have to put on the fake happy faces that everyone wanted to see or pretend we were okay and "getting over it." I recommend the Emmaus Ministry retreats to any other parent grieving the loss of their children, whether preborn or at any age.

CHAPTER 3

JOSH'S UNKNOWN GIFT
OF HOPE TO US

When Abel and I started going to therapy as grieving parents together, we went weekly. In addition to that appointment, we had our own individual therapists. For our grieving parents' therapy, we would go for our appointment with Barry Walsh, our therapist at the Bridge in Worcester, where Erin had worked at the time of the accident, and then go to Josh's to check on him and bring him lunch. Being at the house with Josh made us feel Erin's presence a bit more because her things were still all around the house, and of course, we'd get to see Elainna, their cat, another bond with Erin. We did that for a couple months until we felt it was doing Josh more harm than good. I think talking about Erin and seeing Abel and me—both of our characteristics must have reminded him of Erin—were causing his grief to be worse, so we spread out our visits to longer intervals.

One day, when we arrived at his house and found none of Erin's effects around, we were stunned. Josh had boxed up everything related to Erin and placed it in a safe place upstairs, keeping a large box of special mementos for himself. It was painful to see the house without her things around. Josh, barely able to speak, put some items for us on the kitchen table. He pointed at them and said that among the items were some journals Erin had written before he knew her. He also gave us her Assumption College diploma and her Bible. Josh couldn't have known at the time how special those journals he entrusted to us were. We had known she kept a journal, but we hadn't known how extensive her writings were and how deeply spiritual, especially at the young age of fourteen and fifteen. Since then, we have found numerous notes and letters she wrote that chronicled her life well. She wrote many of her thoughts down, even on scraps of paper. We've only scratched the surface of what is probably packed in boxes and bins that we haven't emotionally managed to get to yet.

Ever since reading the journals Josh gave us, I have had a strong feeling that I must get them published so her faith and, especially, her hope can be shared with as many people as possible. Hope is needed so much in this dark world. I have already distributed well over a hundred copies of just the excerpts of her writings to family, friends, and anyone else who seemed interested. When I finally connected with AuthorHouse to publish Erin's writings, they suggested I add Erin's biography so people who enjoy her writings can further understand her by knowing what she was doing in life at the time of her writings and how her thinking may have developed.

Following the introduction, you can read my favorite excerpt of Erin's, which I felt was just for me, and maybe you will be touched by it too. It was consoling. I believe "Footprints" was one of her favorite poems. What particularly touched me was the last line: "it was then that I carried you." She wrote the phrase "I carried you" in larger letters all by itself. I believe she was somehow letting me know that God carried her out of that car and brought her to His heavenly home, where she is safe and loved immensely.

The following excerpt, written July 20, 2005, at 11:40 p.m., when Erin was a month away from turning fifteen, I believe was meant for Abel's benefit. He has had a difficult and painful time in missing her physical presence. I hope it has helped him and some of her friends deal with their grief. Abel grieves like both a father and a mother. Because of our homeschooling, he spent an unusually large amount of time with Erin, more than most fathers are able to spend with their children, and he developed both motherly and fatherly bonds with her. A few weeks after the accident, Abel mentioned that when he'd seen Erin's upside-down car, he'd felt a physical pain in his heart and had thought of the great sword that pierced the Blessed Mother's heart and the excruciating pain she must have felt in watching her Son be beaten and scourged and die on the cross. Abel identified with her at that moment. We know Mary feels our pain.

7/20/05 11:40pm

   I have been giggling, looking over the pages of my past. Oh, how I wish life would still be like that. But sadly, it is not anymore. As I grew older, I came to find out that the world is a very cold and cruel place. Though, yes it does have it's happy moments. Sadly they are much too little. And very rare. There are many times lately where I find myself feeding off old happy

memories from the past. Being
a child is such a wonderful
time. How I envy those who
are young and I pine to go
back to those times but I
should not live in the past,
or the future, For if we
were to just dwell on memories
or things to come, we would
forget to live and there
waste our entire lives
because of our foolish
desires to try and be
happy even though I
actually believe it to

13

make you feel a lot worse.
So, whoever may be reading
this, do not worry yourself
with things of old or
happy moments that
have come and gone,
but make brand new
ones each second of the
day. Make every moment
very special. Live your
life to the very fullest that
it can possibly be. I
really hope you do. Your's, Erin

14

PART 2

ERIN'S EARLY YEARS

"All is welcome. Yes all is welcome." Say the Lord. All can come to his house in hevine. Oh yes all are welcome to his house.
—as written by Erin Kate Rodriques,
April 12, 2001 (ten years old)

Chapter 4

Preborn and Birth

Abel and I had been married for almost nine years when I finally became pregnant three months before I turned forty. Erin was our miracle child for whom we had been waiting. During the pregnancy, my doctor tested for Down's syndrome. Of course, my numbers came out with a high possibility for Down's due to my age skewing the equation. I declined an amniocentesis for birth defects, as the results would not have changed our minds about continuing the pregnancy, and it possibly could have caused a miscarriage. We knew we would gladly take whatever child God gifted us with. Following is a photo of week thirty-eight of my pregnancy. One photo album covers me at every week of pregnancy, safely carrying Erin within me.

When my due date had come and gone, we went to the hospital for a scheduled nonstress test, and the results showed I was in labor and didn't know it. They tried to induce me for more than twelve hours, but I wasn't dilating much—Erin was too comfy inside—so they performed a cesarean section shortly before midnight on August 17, 1990. I heard the doctors talking and laughing as they watched Erin smile on the other side of my membranes. Erin's warm and tender smile and connection with others began.

Week thirty-eight, safe within.

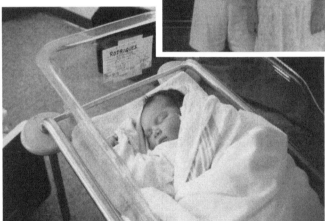

Newborn Erin
ready to meet
the world.

Chapter 5

Infant and Toddler Years

A month after Erin was born, she received the sacrament of Baptism at our local parish of St. Mary in Norton, Massachusetts. The priest, Father Herb Cleary, had been a Jesuit friend of mine for many years. My sister Maureen was her godmother, and Abel's brother Don was her godfather. Abel sang some songs and played the guitar at the celebration. Family and friends came from near and far for the occasion. The priest's parting words to Erin and us were "I send you forth." And so we went. Erin's spiritual quest had begun.

Godparents Uncle Don and Aunt Maureen.

From her day of birth, Abel and I included Erin in every part of our lives, from the sad times to the joyous times. We didn't want to shield her from sad life events; we wanted her to know that those times were also part of life and nothing to be afraid of. When Erin was four, whenever we visited my father in the nursing home, patients and visitors there would give Erin ice cream and stuffed animals. She watched Grammy visit Grandpa at least daily, if not more often, and she saw other dedicated husbands and wives feeding their barely responsive spouses faithfully every day while they chatted joyfully with them and us—such great examples of married love. There were also daughters and sons visiting parents and siblings visiting ill brothers and sisters. In my fear of nursing homes, I thought there would be much sadness, but there was much love—simple yet deep love so overwhelming that it brought tears to my eyes. We wanted Erin to feel like that was a normal part of life. The three of us, along with my mother, were there when my father died. We prayed the Rosary beside his hospital bed and were there when he took his last breath. Similarly, not long after, Erin, Abel, his mother, and other family were there when his grandmother died. Erin attended wakes and funerals with us. She went to many happy occasions with us also—weddings, birthday and anniversary parties, and so on. We wanted her to experience the variety and reality of life so she would be comfortable in it as she grew older. Erin grew up amid large gatherings of family and friends, as Abel is the oldest of sixteen, and I'm the oldest of four. She was surrounded by people of all ages and ethnicities.

We incorporated our faith into our daily living so as to give Erin a solid foundation. We went to Mass regularly on Sundays and holy days and occasionally during the week. Often, we said prayers before meals, before bed, and in the morning individually, and we prayed our Rosary and Chaplet of Divine Mercy as often as we could, sometimes together and sometimes separately. We used the room that probably would have been a formal living room for most as our prayer room and library. Others might refer to theirs as meditation rooms or quiet spaces.

Before bed, I always blessed Erin on the forehead with the sign of the cross and with holy water if it was nearby. I carried on that tradition her whole life, and I still do it now to her picture every night on my way up to bed, telling her that I love her and miss her.

We celebrated our own holy days as well as some of those from other faiths. We had a menorah as well as an Advent wreath to show our connection with our religious history. On Christmas morning, we always had a birthday cake and sang "Happy Birthday" to Baby Jesus before we opened our presents. I taught her to revere God's name and never use it in casual conversation. I told her that the only time "Oh my God" or "Jesus, Mary, and Joseph" should be used was in a prayer. I never heard my own father, who grew up in a rough part of town, swear. He would say, "Jeepers Crackers." That was the extent of his swearing.

We helped out at our parish and in the community. We tried to make it all a natural extension of our faith and not a forced one, not wanting to drive Erin away from it. I don't recall ever feeling that she resented that. She was comfortable in practicing our family and faith traditions. I encouraged Erin to develop a personal relationship with God and talk to Jesus, which it seems she did from her writings, and her closeness to God overflowed into her interactions with others. Every once in a while, I come across lists Erin made with the names of people she was praying for and sometimes even novenas for their specific needs, including friends, relatives, and even politicians and celebrities. Erin was a walk-the-talk person who shared her love and mercy with all she met. Not only from my own observations but also from listening to and reading all the stories people have been telling us, I know that Erin had a special aura about her, an open heart, which I feel was used by God to reach others with His love and mercy.

We purposely had only one television set, which was in the family room. It was our attempt to keep us together and not isolated in separate rooms. PlayStation, Nintendo, and similar diversions were not even considered, as I thought they would be too addicting and time consuming—not just for Erin but for any of us! It didn't seem to bother Erin. She would join in playing video games with others at her friends' or family's houses. Even when I finally broke down her junior year of high school and got a PlayStation—for myself to use for *Dance, Dance Revolution* exercise, though I probably used it twice and then never again—she was minimally interested in it.

Fortunately, she was not into brand-name clothes or items. She wasn't materialistic; she only had a lot of "stuff" because many family and friends gave her gifts for birthdays and holidays. Probably her most favored items were books and all the Lord of the Rings acquisitions in her teen years.

Erin with Mom and Dad

Mother Goose (VoVo-
Lucinda Rodriques)
and her grandchildren
(Erin is in front, the
smallest one under
Barney's left paw).

Several years later,
Erin and her cousins
Kayla and Chantel.

Erin and Dad on an average day.

CHAPTER 6

EARLY CHILDHOOD

Because Abel and I managed to work opposite shifts, one of us was always home with Erin for the first five years. Abel and Erin were well known around our small town because they were seen at the local stores, the post office, and especially the library. Erin began with story time at the library and frequented the library throughout high school, eventually becoming a Junior Friend of the Library. Abel took Erin on many outings to the nearby Audubon Sanctuary trails, and they fished together from the bridge down the street, which overlooks the river that runs deep in the woods behind our house; gardened in our yard; and painted the fences that surrounded our vegetable garden. Erin loved to do busywork and enjoyed being with us and with other kids and adults. Even when she was a young age, I could already see her empathizing with people in her quiet way. She brought people and animals joy and tender care.

Erin attended kindergarten at the J. C. Solmonese School in town, where Mrs. Rosemary Kline was her teacher. Abel volunteered in her classroom every week or so. He remembers Erin coming over to him one day and gently whispering, "Dad, that's not what Mrs. Kline wants you to do. It's this way." She was always looking out for her parents, even as a young child.

After much discussion with friends and family, we decided to homeschool Erin from first grade through high school. Our only concern was the socialization aspect of her being an only child. Well, there was no need to worry about that. Erin had many friends already, as well as many cousins and other family members. She swam and played T-ball at the YMCA, participated in library activities, and continued to accompany Abel or me on our errands around town. She began piano lessons with Rue Siegel around the age of ten because of the influence of her friend Joey, who was three years older. He was already becoming quite accomplished at the piano.

When Abel's and my work shifts coincided, Erin would bring her assignments and spend the day with Joey and his parents, Mary-Jo and Donald, who also homeschooled. Every day was an adventure for them. They took many field trips either by themselves or with the local homeschool group. When they got older, they did square dancing with the group, as well as music and science classes. They also attended Mass most days of the week, usually at LaSalette Shrine in Attleboro.

Erin received the sacrament of Reconciliation (or Penance, or Confession) when she was almost eight. After her first confession, Mary-Jo and Joey were waiting outside church, carrying flowers and wearing gigantic sunglasses. They told Erin she was so holy she was glowing. We all went back to their house to visit Donald, Mary-Jo's husband, who, at that time, was fairly bedridden with multiple sclerosis, though he still had his great sense of humor (that's a whole other book or two!). When we went into the bedroom, he was lying in bed with his oversized sunglasses on too. It was a memorable day.

Reconciliation was followed by receiving her First Communion. Both sacraments were administered by our friend Father Greg Mathias, the same priest who later said Erin's funeral Mass and was supposed to celebrate Josh and Erin's marriage. On the day of her First Communion, there was a torrential downpour. As we ran from the car to the church, the rain strangely stopped briefly until we were inside. A big celebration with family and friends followed the Mass.

Erin's first sacrament of Reconciliation with Father Greg
Mathias. Joining us after were the Spencers.

Erin's First Communion, pictured with her parents, Grammy
Eleanor Scanlon (left), and VoVo-Lucinda Rodriques (right).

Erin and Dad working outside.

Erin, dressed as Blessed Kateri Tekakwitha, getting ready to ride on the Knights of Columbus float.

Erin and Dad.

PART 3

MIDDLE YEARS

That is how I try to make my life. Bring out that light.
To find that little flicker of light in a world that is
full of deep darkness. It is the way I must live.
—Erin Rodriques, December 12, 2005 (fifteen years old)

CHAPTER 7

MIDDLE SCHOOL AND PRETEEN YEARS

Erin and Joey were introduced by Abel to the Star Wars movies. They quickly became taken with them, donning their costumes and lightsabers. They were big movie buffs, and the movies they saw through the years were innumerable. The Pirates of the Caribbean movies were another obsession—Erin was in love with Commodore James Norrington. *It's a Wonderful Life* remained her favorite Christmas movie throughout her whole life. *Master and Commander* was a favorite movie and book. However, the biggest true 24-7 obsession was Tolkien's Lord of the Rings (LOTR) books and movies. I tried to read the books so I could keep up with her, but I was lost in the wide array of characters. I did enjoy the movies. *The Fellowship of the Ring* came out in December 2001, three months after the 9/11 attacks, when Erin was eleven. It was the perfect timing for such a film.

Erin made many worldwide friends through her LOTR love. Many of them were introduced through her soon-to-become friend Anna Gorin's LOTR website, Arwen-Undomiel.com (A-U for short). Erin was a moderator for it for a few years. Erin had friends in Denmark, Australia, Canada, Germany, and several states here—and, of course, Joey. She got to meet a few of them in person. All of them became her lifelong close friends, sharing their personal lives as well as their love for Tolkien.

Around that same time in Erin's life, I was diagnosed with Hodgkin's lymphoma shortly after my fiftieth birthday in 2000. Erin was still about nine when I was diagnosed. She worried about me for all that time and probably forever after. She kept her anxiety hidden during my six months of chemo and radiation treatments. Fortunately, Maxine, our adopted beagle, came into our lives shortly before all that began. Erin could hug and confide in Maxine. As beagles are not man's best friend since they will abandon you and disappear into the woods when they get a tempting whiff of something, Erin probably felt further anxiety every time Maxine escaped her leash.

Erin with Maxine.

Erin with Mom and Dad
at a cousin's wedding.

During that period of my sickness, we continued to homeschool. I had to take a leave of absence from work because the fatigue and fuzzy brain were not conducive to my daily ninety-mile round-trip commute or to my filling prescriptions. Some days were tough when I couldn't even concentrate to watch TV, let alone converse with anyone. On those days, Erin went to Joey's to do her schoolwork, unless my mother, Grammy, was down from Maine and staying with us. Other days, Erin would go to Abel's mother's or his sister Alice's craft store, where she loved to restock shelves and use the cash register. Many days, we were home together, and that's why I considered cancer my gift from God—because I got to spend so much time with Erin. The day before I returned to work, the two of us hugged and sobbed all day. I hated that I could not be at home with her, but we had no choice. Both Abel and I needed to work to meet our bills. My heart broke all the while that I was at work away from her, but as I look back, I am grateful we were able to afford all the special trips and other activities of which we now have wonderful memories and photos. I'm thankful we had those opportunities. I feel now, through some of her writings, that Erin understood that, and she always looked forward to my days off so we could spend them together.

Once my strength returned after the Hodgkin's episode, we made a few extra fun trips to make up for the lost year. One was to Disney World, with a side trip to Discovery Cove, where Erin and Abel swam with the dolphins. That was when she decided she wanted to be a marine biologist.

In July 2002, when Erin was almost twelve, we went to College of the Atlantic Family Summer Camp in Bar Harbor, Maine. We stayed in the dorms there, in bunk beds, constantly hitting our heads on the one above or the ceiling. We met a nice family from Pennsylvania whom Erin adopted quickly. There were many interesting activities, including beaver dams; geologic hikes; and boat rides to see the fjords, puffins, whales, and dolphins, but the most fun one of all was the Dive-In Theater starring Diver Ed, who looked and acted like John Belushi and dressed in an old-fashioned-looking deep-diving suit complete with globe-shaped headgear. He would go down under the boat with his camera and livestream the various creatures onto the TV monitor in the boat. Then he would bring some of the creatures up with him and place them in a tank for everyone to examine. Abel and Erin would probably argue that their favorite time in Bar Harbor was when they rented bikes and explored a nearby tidal island, Bar Island, which had an exposed sandbar during low tide. When they reached the top of the hill on the island, they were looking at the beautiful panoramic view, when, down below, they noticed people running back across the sandbar because the tide was coming in quickly. The two of them raced down the rough terrain, with Erin falling at least once, and then hurried to make it across the sandbar with the water rising quickly. A stranger carried Erin's bike, and Abel, with his bike in one hand, helped her back to the mainland in rushing waist-deep water. The thought was too scary for me, and I'm glad I didn't know about it until they were back at the college safely.

During those years, Erin was still participating in YMCA sports. She enjoyed tennis, track and field, and basketball. With some of her homeschool friends, she belonged to the Junior Rangers of Borderland State Park and square dancing. One of her favorite places continued to be the Norton Public Library, where she was a Junior Friend by then.

Friends' Memories: Joe Spencer[7]

I doubt I could remember all the movies we went to over the years. When Star Wars Episode III came out, we were there, in costume with lightsabers. As we were sitting in our seats, waiting for the movie to start we heard the sounds of someone bumping into people and apologizing. Erin said, "oh gosh," and began to sink into her seat since Abel had come to surprise us. He then accidentally wacked someone in the head with one of the lightsabers. Erin continued to sink further into her seat. There were all the Pirates of the Caribbean movies where Erin would eschew any affection for Will Turner or Jack Sparrow, and would instead talk about how much she loved Commodore Norrington … Erin loved her parents, even when she felt the need to roll her eyes at their behavior … She would always talk about how much fun she had on the family trips to Maine, Block Island, World Youth Day. She loved her parents immensely.

Tennis at the Y.

Erin and Joey at piano recital.

Erin in her Lord of the
Rings costume.

Trip to Discovery Cove.

CHAPTER 8

TEEN YEARS

Just before high school, Erin joined the Edge, a Catholic youth group at St. Mary's Church in nearby Foxboro. She stayed friends all her life with many of the kids from that group. She was only in the Edge for a year before she was old enough to join Lifeteen at that same parish. Once again, she remained friends with the other teens and older core leaders until the day she died. Through Lifeteen, Erin's faith matured and blossomed. I thank Louise in a special way. Louise was a Lifeteen supporter and was the one who encouraged Erin to keep a journal, according to one of Erin's excerpts. Without her encouragement, we might not have had Erin's inspirational writings.

Erin enjoyed the many devotions and activities she participated in, from Eucharistic Adoration, XLT, Lift, and Sunday night Mass to participating in Pizza and Prayer, working on and riding on floats for the Foxboro Founders' Day parades, and going on retreats in Vermont and Cape Cod as well as to Steubenville East conferences with her Lifeteen and homeschool friends. While she was in Lifeteen, Father Jay gave her a book about St. Thérèse of Lisieux, whom he thought Erin could relate to. The book was the third edition of *The Story of a Soul: The Autobiography of St. Thérèse of Lisieux*, translated from the original manuscript by John Clarke, OCD.[1] St. Thérèse was twenty-four when she died in 1897. Little did Father Jay know that Erin and St. Thérèse had more in common than he realized at the time.

Erin inherited a lot of forever sisters and brothers as they talked

---

[1] Washington, DC: ICS Publications, 1996.

about their future plans and dreams as well as their latest woes. She went to P2BC (Proud2BCatholic) with her friends and cousin Kevin and to other concerts, cheering and singing to local and national Christian music groups. She was a loyal, effervescent fan of Zealous, Righteous B, Jon Niven, and Bernie Choiniere, as well as her favorite drummers, Chad Cunningham and Austin Walker, and kept in touch with all of them through the years. Erin loved music. In addition to the piano, she also played the guitar, ukulele, and keyboard.

Friends' Memories: Joe Spencer[8]

Then there were all the Proud 2B Catholic festivals. I lost count of how many times Erin made sure that we were close enough to Righteous B when he was performing so that she had the opportunity for him to sweat on her. I'm not sure if she ever washed one shirt of hers since he had been very near to us and it was a rather warm day. We would always be at the front of the mosh pit, Erin with her huge sunglasses and me with my backwards cap, with our "Thug life" looks on our faces.

Thug Life. Photo credit Joe Spencer.

Erin and Pope Benedict XVI.
Photo credit Patria Ferragamo.

Zealous (Aaron Hostetter) posing with Erin, who was supporting him with her friends (at top). Photo credits Brin Warrenda (top) and Aaron Hostetter (bottom).

Erin and Debbie Andersen.

Erin at Steubenville East.

Mom and Erin at a Lifeteen event.
Photo credits Patrick Logan.

The following page, written on June 27, 2005, at 12:23 a.m., contains Erin's thoughts about Father John leaving Lifeteen because he was being transferred to Methuen, Massachusetts. Father John was a major life force in the Lifeteen group. He was a down-to-earth yet deeply spiritual man with a great sense of humor and involvement with the teens. His departure was a major loss for the group.

Father John McLaughlin with Erin and her mom and dad at Father John's farewell party.

6/27/05 12:23AM
Tonight was a tough night
I had to say goodbye to one
of the most important people in
my life. A great role model
and father. One I could always
go to when I needed help and
guidance. Some one I could
trust my life with. Someone
who is sent from God. This
special someone is Father John.
Tonight was his last Mass
and his farewell party. I cried.
I can't remember when the last
time it was that I cried. Tonight
was very emotionally straining
but I need to keep thinking
positive. That is the key to a better
and happier life. Just sometimes
it is so hard. Like lately.

High school was packed with many exciting adventures for Erin. She was still obsessed with Lord of the Rings and corresponded daily with her worldwide LOTR friends. She had many lasting, close relationships with them, and now Abel and I are connected to them. I recall a day when we went to the Boston Museum of Science to see the LOTR exhibit and get the autograph of Sean Astin, who played Sam in the LOTR movies. When we got there, they had already cordoned off the line for Sean because it had reached the limit. That didn't discourage Erin. She had brought a football—as in his movie *Rudy*—and some other items for him to sign. She didn't give up. She kept jumping into the line every time the security guard turned around—and the security guard continued to throw her out of the line. She was practically hanging from the ceiling in trying to get in. That was not like Erin. Finally, she started asking people on the other side of the rope to take her items to get his signature. She was trusting. They actually did get his signature and returned her items to her. My faith in mankind was restored! When the girl carrying her football was talking to Sean, she told him that Erin was donating the signed football to Lifeteen for a raffle. When he heard that, he gestured to Erin and gave her a wave. She was thrilled. The little, quiet Erin struck again. Her only disappointment that day was in not managing to meet up with Taryn, one of her LOTR friends from Canada. Somehow, our paths didn't cross. By the way, she did actually donate—I'm sure with inner pain—the football to the Lifeteen raffle.

At the end of her sophomore year, she made her Confirmation at St. Timothy's Church in Norwood, Massachusetts, where she had been helping out with their youth ministry. Her Confirmation sponsor was Marie Lucci from Foxboro Lifeteen. Erin looked up to Marie, who was a great faith and life example to her.

Erin was confirmed by Cardinal Sean O'Malley. Marie Lucci, her sponsor, is standing next to her. Kathy and Abel are on the right.

Three months later, Abel, Erin, and I joined St. Mary's Lifeteen on their pilgrimage to World Youth Day in Cologne, Germany. It was the first time any of the three of us had been to Europe. Erin was in heaven! She had always loved everything European, so she was in her glory. We arrived in Munich and boarded the tour bus. We visited Neuschwanstein Castle; the concentration camp in Dachau, which was sobering; awesomely beautiful churches and cathedrals in Munich and Cologne; and much more. Erin celebrated her fifteenth birthday in Düsseldorf, where we were staying during our time in Cologne. Abel found a man we joked was his twin, or rather, his twin found him. He was a man from Ukraine. Everyone was snapping pictures of the two. The resemblance was uncanny. I would insert their picture, but there's no way to get his twin's permission.

As usual, Erin made many new friends. She made friends from the USA as well as other countries, including Brazil, Italy, and Portugal, on packed—nearly spine-severing—trains (she and her friends searched the internet for one nameless cute guy from Italy to no avail) and on the field where we slept the night before Pope Benedict's outdoor Mass. The field went on and on seemingly without end, with wall-to-wall people. The next day, with Erin carrying or wearing her newly acquired flags of Brazil and Portugal, we began the long trek from the field back to the bus—about ten miles. She still had energy. Me? Not so much. Thank you, Patrick, for carrying my backpack most of the way back!

Erin at World Youth Day, Cologne, Germany, 2005. Photo credits Patrick Logan.

Abel walking behind Erin.

These next pages were written in December 2005, before Christmas, just four months after we had returned from Germany. In Erin's dark times, she would look for any "little scraps of hope" until she could "see the world in a most beautiful light."

SpongeBob, a character from a famous Nickelodeon cartoon, must have been a "flicker of light" for her. Look for the light!

In the second entry, you can see the special kind of relationship she had with God—down to earth and personal. I wonder if she was aware of the promises God put in her heart.

trying to keep my spiritual high up but it is so hard sometimes. You know, sometimes this world seems like a dark and empty place and you can see some of the worst things in it and eventually it looks completely hopeless and you feel so alone in a world of sin and doubt. But, then, you search, and you find little scraps of hope and you continue to hold onto them and eventually you see the world in a most beautiful light and you are so full of hope and you find reasons to live, reasons to go on. When I find myself looking at the world in a dark and dreary way, I look for those good pieces of hope and I do find them. and it fills me with such an unimaginable feeling It's so wonderus and amazing. That is how I try to make my life. Bring out that light. To find that little flicker of light in a world that is full of deep darkness. It is the way I must live. If I didn't I have no Idea how I would be able to survive in a

place like this. Well,
sorry about the deepness!
Off to go watch Spongebob!!
And yes I did write
all this deep stuff
while I was watching
Spongebob on tv. :)

12/20/05 11:46 pm
  Sorry I haven't said much. Been ~~totally~~ busy with the Christmas season. Next year I starting Christmas shopping, decorating and cleaning in October! ~~@~~. Time has gone by ~~there~~ unbelievably fast and I have barley had time to take a breath! Internet isn't working... no idea how

I'm going to survive!
I really need to work
on my relationship with
God. I'm still totally
religious and spread the
word but I think that
I have been trying too
much to help others with
their relationship with
God that I have
barely been paying attention
to mine. I think tonight,
instead of saying the Rosary,
I'm going to just talk to
Jesus and pray for
peace, strength and help.
I know He will not
abandone me. Lord, I
know you can read this
and you know me better

then I know myself,
please know I love
you more than anything
in this world and my
desire for you is so
strong that when I
feel like I haven't
talked to you for even
just one day, I feel dead.
I need to remember
to place all my stresses
and worries into your
hands and have you
help me and guide
me along my life's
path. I love you
Lord and I need you.
Please be always at
my side and help me
even when I do not

think to ask. I can never thank you enough for all that you have done for me.

The following writing, for me, was profound and comforting. It was written on May 26, 2006, when she was still fifteen years old, just before she began practicing for the Connecticut Renaissance Faire and at the end of a big change at Lifeteen with several adult CORE members moving on: "and if it is not His will for us to meet again on this earth than [sic] we shall all definitely meet in the next life and it will be the greatest thing to ever happen."

I'm looking forward to that "greatest thing to ever happen" time when we will see her again.

I know that He can even change
our thoughts and stuff so I'm starting
to have this great feeling that everything is going to be okay. I love
You Jesus so much. You help
me in so many great ways that
I could never tell it all. Bernie
is now music minister at St. Monica's
so he will be leaving Foxboro at
the end of June. He announced
it last Sunday and made this
beautiful speech but I already
knew it was going to happen because
he told me about 4 months ago.
Mike and Danni are leaving,
they announced it right before
Bernie but Mike had also told
me last Thursday during the
end of XLT so I knew. Gail
also announced she was leaving

last Sunday as well but I
had already heard that around
last September. So none was a
surprise but it was still hard for
me to see it. But we are all
placing it in God's hands. If
it is His Will, we shall be
together someday on this earth
and if it is not His Will for us
to meet again on this earth
than we shall all definitely
meet in the next life and it will
be the greatest thing to ever
happen.

Please ignore the thing on the
next page, Tommy M. and I were
play scrabble on the way to
Neushwanstien. :)
The next page was when I was teaching
Joe on the plane.

A month later came an entry wherein Erin expresses gratefulness amid confusion and feeling "weird."

Thank, hope, and trust to get through your times of confusion.

June 12th, 2006 11:39 pm
I feel so confused and weird
right now but I just have to trust in
God that everything is going to be okay.
Right now my life is crazy but it
looks that way by the light I am
holding it in, the world's way. Instead,

I need to look at it in God's way and when I do, my life looks really great and full of such hope. So right now I'm going to write down some things that happened today that I am very thankful for to God. I am thankful to be alive this day. I am thankful for being alive. I am thankful for getting to watch Frasier. I am thankful for getting to spend some time with my mom. I am thankful for it being nice weather. I am thankful for getting to go to Pizza and prayer. I am thankful for getting to sit next to Derek. I am thankful for every one who was there. I am thankful for getting to see and talk

to Cesco. I am thankful for getting
to eat good popcorn tonight! I am
thankful for getting to talk to
Kit and others that I talked to.
I am thankful that I got to
post on my Xanga. I am thankful
that Cesco commented on my
MySpace. I am thankful for
getting to upload all my pictures.
I am thankful for everything!!!
God, please help me through this
time and to see each day
with hope and trust. Amen.

Sept. 14th, 2006 12:12 AM
    Wow! It's been awhile since I last
wrote in here. Let me update you on my
crazy life. :/ A LOT has changed, I must
warn you. Let's see what has happened
since then... Okay, I might forget something

Three months later, in September 2006, when she was sixteen, Erin wrote about some summer activities and the high school graduation of a few Lifeteen friends.

Founder's Day/Voice Recital/ FHS Graduation.

So on June 17th it was Founder's Day, it rained like crazy. We still marched in the parade... though ~~my~~ ¹? Life Teen's Float that we worked so hard on was melting. We were soaked to the bone. After, everyone went off to work at the LT booth where the festivities were being held ~~at~~ the big parking lot ~~of~~ the Foxboro Company. I didn't go. I had to race home, get washed and dressed and run out to my voice recital. I must admit that it was rather long and a bit torturous. When it was my turn, the songs I had aced earlier, I failed. There were many, many spotlights so I couldn't see at all. And one of my weird things is, when I can't see, I can't do anything. Guh.. So annoying... after that... I forgot what happened... what did happen!? I know the second half of Founder's Day was postponed to the next day. Anyways, let's just move on. :) Next day I got all dressed up again and went alone to the Foxboro Graduation. I got some wonderful shots of Alex, Joe and Jen!!! It was a beautiful graduation and one of the greatest days I have seen

 in my whole life. Then I went to LifeTeen Mass. After that was Mark's first LifeNight. THEN! The night I had been waiting for! Founder's Day! We had a crazy night. Got great pictures, too!

Must sleep. Night.

Dec. 11th(7), 2006 at 12:18 AM

WoW! Again, long time, no talk. Lemme quickly get you updated on the situation while I should be sleeping.

In the summer of 2006, Erin auditioned for a part in the Connecticut Renaissance Faire in Hebron, Connecticut. She got the role of the barkeep's daughter, Brigit. She enjoyed the Renaissance Faire members, especially Roderick Russell, the sword swallower; the Brigands, a pirate musical group; and the many Erics, Ehrichs, and Erichs who were the owner, gypsies, musicians, juggler, weasel, vendor, and more. She kept in touch with many of them too. The years before and after she was a cast member, she dragged us there almost every weekend of the fall while they were performing, and she dressed as a pirate or fair maiden. She always loved to be in costume, whether dressed as an elven princess, Princess Leia from *Star Wars*, or Blessed (now Saint) Kateri Tekakwitha or wearing her Renaissance Faire dresses.

Dancing with her Faire friend.
Photo credit Eric Tetreault.

Erin and her friend Roderick
Russell, a famous hypnotist
and *Guinness Book of World
Records* sword swallower.
Photo credit Eric Tetreault.

Erin and her LOTR and homeschool
friend from Maine, Hannah Peterson.

More photos of Erin at the Renaissance Faire. Photo credit Eric Tetreault.

In the middle of Erin's junior year of high school, Erin asked to meet with a therapist to help with her anxiety. With Father Greg's recommendation, we found one. Clara, her therapist, met regularly with Erin; their goals of treatment were to discuss Erin's college choices, reduce her dislike of telephones, explore patterns of her relationships, and help Erin with appropriate argumentation. Erin basically needed an unrelated person to vent to. She had some anxiety and depression but was able to keep it together on the outside. Erin continued to see therapists when she was in college and after graduation.

I can't forget her Josh Groban obsession. July 27, 2007, just before the beginning of her last year in high school, Abel and I took Erin and her friend Kristen to see Josh Groban in Manchester, New Hampshire. What a show he put on! I think I lost my hearing there; the screams were deafening! A couple times during his show, he appeared at the top of a stairway in the audience and walked down through the people. Amazingly, despite our being among a crowd of thousands, he stood at the top of our aisle and gradually walked toward the front. When he got to our row, he stopped, looked over, and waved directly at Erin, as if acknowledging her, as if there were a connection. It was a strange moment. Everyone around us commented on it. It certainly made her night! Today it comforts me when I hear him sing "To Where You Are." Maybe he's still connected to Erin.

When I was reviewing Erin's Facebook to make sure I had downloaded any photos I needed for the book, I came across a post Erin wrote a couple of weeks after the concert:[9]

> Okay brace yourself people….During his Awake tour, when he sings "In Her Eyes" the lights always go out and then he pops out of somewhere in the crowd….and guess what!!!!!!! HE PICKED US!!! So he came right down the aisle, looks at me, points at me, smiles at me, and sings to me!!!!!!!! I was in Heaven!!!!!!! Did I take a picture of him doing [it]? Of course not because I was screaming and passing out.

The next journal entry is a "random moment" of Erin's on August 10, 2007, a week before her seventeenth birthday. This piece—in which she talks about Anne Frank—is one of the reasons I know that Erin wouldn't mind my sharing her writings with others. She wonders if anyone will read her journals in the future and relive her life, maybe laughing and crying over her entries.

For reference, the Winterfeast she talks about in the entry was a celebration that the members of the Connecticut Renaissance Faire attended in Charlton, Massachusetts.

matter how hard I try. Though
I must admit, I am not trying
my hardest *Random moment* I wonder
will anyone ever read this? Look back
on my life. Perhaps laugh and cry
with me as they relive my life with
the help of this and my other journals.
Maybe I'll be famous someday
and after I am dead and
gone this shall be up for grabs
on eBay. If ebay is even around
by then. Though it's all about money
so it probably will still be
around. Did Anne Frank ever
realize her diary would be published
years later for millions, even billions
of people to read, inspire, study, write
essays on, make movies of, have
Broadway productions of? Probably.
Funny isn't? Well, I still can't

think of anything that has ~~be~~ happened
in January so I guess I will move
on to February. This was the second
to last time I saw Cesco (Last
time was two months later in April.)
The Mello's Re~~treat~~ center burned
down. I think that was one of those
very heartbreaking moments where you
actually feel like you lost a part of
yourself. "Never whole again, are we?"
   For some reason that quote keeps
repeating it self in my head. It really
strikes me. Not sure the exact reason
why but I expect it's because I can
relate to it and am so blown away
by the truth to it. And yes, I know
it's the line Barty Crouch Sr. says
to Harry in the 4th

movie. I'm a nerd.
Sue me. Actually,

a part of me wants to say it was in March but I'm still not sure. Anyways, late February-early March. March was actually an eventful month, I went to Winterfeast which was of course wonderful. I got to see almost all my old faire friends and it was certainly a great night of fantastic fun! March was also the month I went to my first Josh Groban concert!!!!! Best concert of my life! Josh is just so amazing, there are not even words that have been invented to tell of what a truly awesome person he is! I think in a few years after I go to college and graduate with an amazing degree, I'll marry him and we'll live happily ever

after. If only life was so easy.
Though, I guess you never know?
I'm sure God has something
great instore for me. ☺
   Alright, I need to sleep even
though I don't want to but
I have to do what is right for
me I guess. "What is right and
what is easy" Wow, okay, I
will stop randomly throwing
out HP quotes. It's starting
to scare me. ☺ Anyways, I
really hope I get to write here
again soon... I actually really
want. Maybe I've gotten over
my fear or whatever strange
quirk I had was. Writing in
this has actually made me
feel more healthy.. Yay!
   Okay, I'm finally leaving.
        Gimighi!

Erin in her Josh Groban shirt and a close up of her angel
wing earrings. Photo credit Anna Gorin.

Lord of the Rings web friends. Top picture, left to right: Patria Ferragamo, Erin, Hannah Peterson, and Anna Gorin. Photo credit Patria Ferragamo. Bottom picture: Kelly "Kit" Le and Erin. Photo credit Kelly Le.

Erin's seventeenth birthday party. Top photo: Erin with
Joe Spencer, a LOTR and homeschool friend.

From top left, clockwise: Erin playing guitar in 2008 (photo credit Anna Gorin); Erin at Cape Cod Lifeteen retreat (photo credit Patria Ferragamo); Erin and Buddy at Dumaine's Retreat Center in Vermont (photo credit Patria Ferragamo); and Cape Cod Lifeteen retreat: Erin Mitchell, Stephanie Storer, Joe Erhard, Erin, Shauna Callahan, and Shannon Ballou (photo credit Katy Bouffard).

Another entry, from December 10, 2007, when Erin was seventeen years old and a senior in high school, is about recognizing blessings in hard times. As Erin says, God's "blessings become more visable [sic] to the average human mind" during hard times.

12/10/07

Lord, I have so much to be thankful for these days. ~~Your~~ Your blessings are so numerous that I could never count them all. During these last few days I have endured some hard times but I believe that during these times your blessings become more visable to the average human mind. Especially last night. When the news of my aunts passing came to me. I found myself with a friend

that was there to be my shoulder to cry on. (or rather me sobbing and him holding me tightly) I have been blessed with so many gifts for having people who care so much about me and help me get through life.

Thank you Jesus.!!

In April 2008, shortly before Erin graduated from high school, Joey's father, Donald, died. As I said earlier in the book, writing about Donald would be a whole other book (or two). In his younger days, before we knew him, I guess he was a wild one in our town. Stories still abound about his escapades. He was diagnosed with multiple sclerosis four years before he and Mary-Jo were married. He worsened fairly rapidly, and by the time we knew him, he first was able get around in an electric wheelchair and then, eventually, was confined to bed. He had his own conversion story through all of it. Donald had a big impact on everyone who walked into his room. From friends and family to health-care staff, everyone had his or her special relationship with him. He loved Erin as his own. He was a great adviser and counselor with an added fantastic sense of humor. As sick as Donald was, there wasn't a dry eye at his funeral. I have no doubt he is causing trouble in Heaven as we speak.

In June, Abel, Erin, and I, along with Grammy and Erin's cousin Kevin, drove to Annapolis, Maryland, to attend her cousin Michael's graduation from the Annapolis Naval Academy. It was a spectacular event complete with the Blue Angels flying over the field. We were able to spend a little time with my brother and his wife, Michael's brother Greg, and some of the family. We toured the campus and also visited the Basilica of the Immaculate Conception in Washington, DC, on our way home. Both were awesome.

Cousin Michael's graduation from Annapolis Naval Academy. Left to right: cousins Erin, Kevin Upham, and Michael and Gregory Scanlon.

Erin and Michael.

The four cousins at a much earlier time.

Top: Greg, Mike, and Erin in younger days. Bottom: Erin at Kevin's
graduation from St. Joseph's College (Maine) in 2005.

Visiting the Basilica of the Immaculate Conception in Washington,
DC, after the Annapolis graduation. Top: Abel, Erin, and Kathy.
Bottom: Kevin Upham, Erin, and Grammy (Eleanor Scanlon).

A couple months after Donald's death and Erin's high school graduation, Abel, Erin, and I again went on a pilgrimage, this time to Medjugorje in Bosnia-Herzegovina, the site of apparitions of the Blessed Mother. Once again, Erin celebrated her birthday on foreign soil, this time her eighteenth. We went with a group from St. Monica's in Methuen, Massachusetts, where Father John McLaughlin—the same Father John who was Erin's Lifeteen priest in Foxboro—was pastor. Our group was staying at a private house in the village, the Pansion St. Michael, which was owned by Vesna R. and her family. Vesna made sure Erin had a beautiful homemade birthday cake. Vesna also helped Erin when she developed a two-day migraine. I don't know what it was, but Vesna had some medication (not labeled in English) that eventually gave Erin some relief. I believe the trigger for the migraine was the day she and Abel joined a few others to climb the rocky Cross Mountain. I knew it was too much for me, so I stayed at the Pansion. The temperature was in the low hundreds, and I'm sure Erin, in her excitement, was not hydrating enough. Between the heat and having to get up so early to leave, I imagine that was the migraine trigger. Sadly, migraines were not a rare thing for Erin. I believe she had a bit of anticipatory anxiety too. She would excitedly wait for an event to happen—a party, the Renaissance Faire, or a concert, for example—and then when the day finally came, she would inevitably have a migraine, nausea and vomiting, or both. Usually, somehow, she still managed to go enjoy herself.

Once again, Erin made new friends on that trip. She loved everyone, never judging; she was a great listener and empathizer.

Erin on pilgrimage in Medjugorje, Bosnia-Herzegovina, August 2008.

The following entry was written in 2008, just after Erin's high school graduation and before we went to Medjugorje. She would have been almost eighteen. Erin and some friends attended the New England Lifeteen Camp in Charlton, Massachusetts. At the beginning of her entry, she quotes part of the song "Quiet Enough," which was written by Jon Niven and appears on his *Show the World* album.[10]

The quote on her second page, in which she mentions being busy, refers to a small poster I had had in my room since I was in college. Erin's heart was attracted to it, and my poster became a constant on her wall instead of mine. Further on in the passage, the way she speaks of eternity is comforting to me. She expresses no concern or fear about it. She was looking forward to that day of living in the love, joy, and happiness God intended for us. I am happy for her and sad for us, but I look forward with strong hope to being united with her again and getting big hugs from her.

"The only time, I'm quiet enough to listen is when I'm sleeping. I don't make time for you because I'm so scared. Scared to know what You have to say, Lord. Please don't let me miss, Your fingerprints..."

Lord I want to serve You and I want to do what You want me to do but the thing that holds me back is that I don't know what You want. I know You leave little hints and signs for people but I'm so blind Lord. I need huge blinking neon in your face signs. When I don't know what You want, I get so concerned and then am not confident in doing what I finally decide in case it's not what You wanted. Please Lord, I am Your loving servant. I place my burdens, my sins, and my heart at Your feet. Please Lord, also know that when I pray.

I really do love you I'm sorry
for all the times when I thought
you weren't there. And when it looks
as if I'm wrapped up in the world
still know that you are my number
one now and always, for eternity.
    "Lord thou knowist I shall be
busy this day. I may forget thee,
do not forget me."

    Eternity... Oh! How I cannot
wait to spend it with you!
    But Lord, one of my biggest
fears in this last universe is
that when I go to enjoy
eternity with you, that not
all of my loved ones will be
there too. Please Lord, hear my
prayers for their souls. For I
know that if they truly, really
knew you that they too

would love you with their
whole hearts.
    Awaiting the day til we finally
see face to face...

    With great Love,
            Your daughter Erin

The following page I found in a spiral notebook of Erin's. From the content of the rest of the notebook, it appears this might have been written at her last high school senior retreat. I think it might have been an assignment, possibly regarding how those who attended the retreat would want to be remembered. Again, you will get a taste of her humor and imagination.

My Obituary

Erin was a Kind and gentle person. She touched many peoples' lives. Not only a gifted musician at piano, guitar, drums, bass, harp and ukulele; she was also heavily involved in helping animals. As a naturalist, she traveled the world ~~discovery~~ exploring, taking care of animals and spreading awareness about the environment trying to follow in the footsteps of her hero, Steve Irwin. Her greatest joy was being able to be part of exhibition to the Galapogos Islands. Erin also was a devout Catholice and was a youth minister, she was very active in youth ministry. She also traveled to third world countries helping those in need. Erin is survived by a loving husband, a number of children, close family and loving friends.

She also was part of the group that banned whaling in the South Pacific.

Most of her journals Josh gave us were written during her high school years. I just wanted to give you an idea of what Erin was involved in during that time period. I tried to refrain from giving you too many of my own interpretations of her messages, leaving it up to you to determine what they could mean for you in your own life.

PART 4

YOUNG ADULT YEARS

Quiet prayer for me is what gave me the greatest
hope. Speak to God, even if you don't think He's
there, don't worry, He's just quietly listening.
—Erin Rodriques, probably written in
the fall of 2010 (age twenty)

Chapter 9

College Years

Not long after we returned from Medjugorje, it was time for Erin to leave for college. Ugh! The day was finally here. Abel and I drove Erin to Worcester, Massachusetts, and moved her into Assumption College. We had many of the usual parental fears, but in addition, after homeschooling for twelve years, I was concerned about how Erin would adjust to a formal classroom, and we were worried for her health and safety because we wouldn't be there to hover over her every second of the day. Well, she hit the ground running and just sent us on our way. She was ready. She didn't seem to have any fears about her new home, at least outwardly. Abel and I, on the other hand, were pretty sad and lonely all the way home and for the next four years.

Two practical indirect results of Erin's homeschooling that helped her in college, I feel, were her (1) having the ability to get along and feel comfortable with people of all ages and (2) not feeling inhibited about sitting up front in class or conversing with her teachers. Of course, the second one got her some negative feedback from a few of the students, I'm sure, but it also enabled her to approach her teachers to get further assistance in understanding her assignments. She became lifelong friends with many of her teachers.

Before Erin graduated from high school, I had her tested for ADHD at the hospital where I worked. One of the brain researchers there told me he wasn't diagnosed until college, and he suggested Erin get tested before then so she would be able to request special assistance at college if needed. Erin always felt she had a learning disability, but her doctor didn't want to pursue testing because she felt Erin had compensated for it with her own way of learning and coping.

Erin's test results showed a diagnosis of ADHD, inattentive type. Some dyslexia was apparent. With that diagnosis, Erin received the proper reports to bring to the office of disabilities at Assumption, where she received academic support services and learned organizational and planning skills. She was also provided with letters to give to her professors to allow her extra time in some cases or use a recorder in others. I think that most of the time, she didn't give the teachers her letter because she was embarrassed to get special treatment. That's just my thought. She still did well in her classes. She loved to learn new things, and that made the difference. I'm sure she had no special interest in a few of her required classes, but she still managed to get good grades in them.

The report also recommended that Erin continue with her therapist for her transition to college as well as begin with a new therapist at Assumption, which she did. The report specifically said that Erin was anxious, tended to internalize and obsess over stress, and would benefit from learning how to identify the stressors and anxious feelings and address them (e.g., with coping skills and organization). She needed to learn how to advocate for herself by building her confidence and self-esteem and address her interpersonal anxiety. The evaluation showed Erin to be a creative and sensitive young woman with a number of important psychological strengths that would help her in that quest. She had a well-developed imagination. The assessment also noted that Erin told them that she "focuses on positives" and said, "[I] remind myself how lucky I am."

In the fall of her freshman year, she became quite sick, unbeknownst to us. I was at work one day and got a call from Erin from the back of an ambulance. She weakly spoke, telling me that the health services nurse had told her to call me to tell me they were transporting her by ambulance to St. Vincent's Hospital in Worcester. She said that she was dying, and her body was eating itself! I sped from Belmont to Worcester and circled the neighborhoods until I found the right hospital. When I found her in the ER, she looked pathetic lying there with her tiny body hooked up to IVs. I was glad to see her boyfriend at the time at her bedside. I knew he would watch over her. When the ER doctor showed me a copy of her labs, I thought she had leukemia or some other serious illness. He said that her numbers were off due to dehydration and that she had the flu, as many others had. She was discharged that day, and I took the both of them back to school, but she wouldn't come home with me. She said she would be fine, and her friends would be there to take care of her.

She ended up calling Abel and me back up the next day because all her friends were in class. While we were there, she was still fatigued and also developed a flat pink rash all over her torso. She had an appointment at health services the next day. In the meantime, I got in touch with her doctor's office back home, and they ordered further tests for her. I asked them to add a Lyme disease test, as she had recently been on a science field trip in the woods. It just so happened that shortly before that, Abel had attended a Lyme documentary and seminar that was pretty frightening, "Lyme: The New Epidemic." On the bloodwork order, the nurse or doctor wrote at the bottom "Mother requests Lyme test," which I interpreted as "I know it doesn't make sense, but the mother requests it." The test came back positive, and Erin was treated for three weeks with doxycycline. She still had some residual joint pain and hand tremors. They declined a bit, but she continued to have them.

She later told me that prior to telling me that she was dying and that her body was eating itself, she had been vomiting all weekend, and when she was in the dorm bathroom, her sight went black. She got down on the floor and crawled back to her room. Apparently, no one was in the dorm; they probably were at class. She managed to call security for a ride to health services. Erin said that according to policy, they couldn't just open her dorm door; they had to wait until she opened it. She felt too sick to get to the door, but fortunately, she mustered up some strength and finally managed to open it. When they dropped her at health services, the receptionist told her she was late for her appointment and had her go lie down in an exam room for what felt like an hour to her. When the nurse practitioner came in to see her, she took one look at her and called the ambulance. The ambulance crew did an EKG on her in the ambulance before they left. I imagine she was incoherent at that point, so whatever was said made her think that she might die because she had waited too long to seek help and that she was so dehydrated that her body was eating itself since it had no other nutrients coming in.

Fortunately, she lived through that ordeal. After the next couple years, still plagued with various infections, frequent colds, migraines, and joint pain, Erin began to see a specialist in Lyme and other environmental illnesses, who was convinced the Lyme organisms were causing her ongoing issues. She was still working with him at the time of the accident, so we'll never know if that's what it was for sure. Most likely, it was chronic Lyme that she had probably had for quite some time. We had been going to Audubon sanctuaries for walks for years, and she acted and volunteered at the Connecticut Renaissance Faire in the thickly wooded areas. At home, we have deer wandering through our yard. I would not be surprised if she had been bitten by ticks throughout the years. The unique bull's-eye rash only shows up in some cases. I don't know how she managed to accomplish so much during those years when she felt so lousy. She had amazing stamina. When she would have a migraine at work, she would go into the bathroom, throw up, and return to her desk again with barely a change in her pleasant demeanor. I would have called in sick and moaned and groaned in bed all day! Once in a while, however, she did have to retreat to bed in a dark, quiet room, unable to function.

During Erin's first couple years and then throughout her time at Assumption, she became involved in Campus Ministry, which made my maternal heart smile, and the school newspaper *Le Provocateur*, better known as the *Provoc*. She became their first art and photo editor and was seen all around campus with her camera. We have photos of Erin with some form of camera in her hand from the time she was three years old. I guess that because we were always taking pictures of her, she wanted to do it too. Professor Mike Land, the *Provoc*'s adviser, became a lifelong good friend. He told us that she had a "keen artistic eye." He, being a photographer also, would inevitably meet up with her around campus at the same photo ops, or they would discuss each other's shots taken at the Wachusett Meadow Trail or elsewhere—same subjects, different times. She continued with both Campus Ministry and the *Provoc* all through college, adding on acting beginning her junior year.

She and her close friends had a ritual of going to Newport, Rhode

Island, for their Winter Study Days every year. Erin loved Rhode Island and the ocean. Most of her relatives from Abel's side of the family live in Rhode Island, so she spent much time there for family parties and events, just as she did with my side of the family on the Maine coast. Abel took pride in the fact that Erin used to take her friends to many places we used to go to together. It confirmed to him that she had appreciated and enjoyed our time together.

For some reason, Erin chose three different places to have her major discussions with me. The first place was in the car, the second was while grocery shopping, and the third was in one of our bathrooms. When one of us was in the shower, the other one would sit on top of the toilet cover while we had big conversations. One day sticks out in my head. It was sometime during Erin's college years—I can't remember when. I was at the sink, getting ready, and she was hovering behind me. She told me that of the three of us, she wanted to be the one to die first, because she was afraid she couldn't live without us. She valued our advice and love. I said, "It's not natural for the child to die first, and you'd better not go before us, or I'll just be crazy for the rest of my life." I told her she had many friends and family members around to be with her. She still insisted how lost she would be. Many times even before that, when she was younger, I had recurring thoughts that Erin was such a good soul—almost not of this world and too good for it—that I always carried the fear that she would die young. Unfortunately, her wish and my fear came true, although I think she would have preferred a later time in life.

In May of Erin's sophomore year, 2010, she had the opportunity to go to France and Italy with the college for ten days. Father D'Alzon's 200th Birthday Celebration Pilgrimage followed in the footsteps of the Assumptionists' founder, Father Emmanuel D'Alzon. The pilgrimage consisted of about thirty travelers: a priest, alumni, faculty, trustees, a handful of students, and the president of the college, President Francesco "Prez Chez" Cesareo. Erin was thrilled to be back in Europe again, in countries she loved and hadn't traveled to before. One of her best friends, Chris Moran, and one of her favorite professors, D'Alzon expert Christian Gobel, were fellow pilgrims, so I'm sure dramatic adventures abounded. Christian fondly remembers that one night in Rome, we went out to dinner together; … Erin, Chris, me and two or three of the Bayard people. I still see us sitting there outside this pizzeria in Trastevere, waiting for the food to arrive, discussing something (probably just pondering life in general) and enjoying "la vita Romana" around us … It's just this general memory of a placid, happy moment.[11]

Erin tried to stay in Prez Chez's group, as he was an expert in Italian history. Prez Chez told me later that they thought Erin was lost for a while at the Coliseum. Apparently, she had gone on with another group touring in a different section. Fortunately, it ended well.

Photo credits Chris Moran.

Before Erin left on the pilgrimage, cancer struck me again. I was diagnosed with breast cancer shortly after my sixtieth birthday. I had already had one surgery before she went on the trip. After she returned, I had to have another surgery in June, as the doctors said I had already had my lifetime amount of radiation from my Hodgkin's treatment in 2000, and a mastectomy followed by tamoxifen was the best route to go. While I was recovering from my second surgery, Abel had an emergency cardiac triple-bypass surgery at the end of July, so poor Erin got stuck taking care of the two of us during her summer break. She and I drove daily up the Southeast Expressway and back to check on Abel while he was recovering in Boston Medical Center for about a week. Prior to the surgery, the only symptom he had was an occasional shortness of breath and a "strange" feeling. Erin kept after him to go to the doctor to have it checked. He finally listened to her (he never listens to me!) and went to the doctor for testing. All his tests appeared normal until they did a cardiac catheterization. The doctor was shocked to see so much blood vessel blockage. He immediately had Abel transferred by ambulance to Boston. I drove my car to pick up Erin at home, and we trekked to Boston to find out what was happening. Before I picked Erin up, Abel had already called her from the ambulance while still medicated and told her that he was probably dying and that he loved her—and where he had hidden some cash. Poor Erin, living with the two of us—no wonder she had anxiety!

I'm sure she was glad to return to college in mid-August for her junior year and to work on the freshman issue of the *Provoc*. She was concerned about leaving us alone, though. It must have been hard to be an only child, especially with older-than-usual parents. She left us a checklist of dos and don'ts: turn off the gas on the stove, turn on the lights outside, and more. We still have her list hanging on our bathroom wall to this day, as you can see following this. The photo with it was taken when Erin was sixteen. In the picture, she has one hand on each of us. As a friend pointed out to us, she was watching over us then, and she is still watching over us closely today.

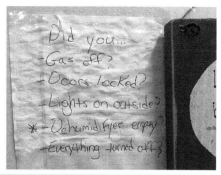

In the fall semester of her junior year, Erin took a photography class with a classmate Freymers Beaubrun. In a recent email, he shared with me a beautiful description of Erin, along with some photos he had taken for the class.

> Your daughter was a wellspring of positivity; the quintessential sweetheart. The limited time I spent interacting with her was nothing but pleasant. I'm sure I'm not the only one to say something similar about her. There was a kindness that radiated from her soul that even strangers could see. My hope is that the photo I took that winter morning captured even 1% of that.[12]

Collage of a sunrise photo shoot at Assumption in December 2010.
Original photo credits Freymers Beaubrun.

Also that fall, Erin had her first college acting role in Tom Dudzick's comedy *Don't Talk to the Actors*, produced by Merely Players, a small theater group at school. She did an outstanding job. We couldn't believe it was Erin onstage—we hadn't known she had it in her. Back in high school, she had performed in piano and voice recitals. She appeared to be self-assured in her piano performances, but she was timid in her singing. She had a pretty voice but didn't project it. She thought she was projecting it, but it wasn't getting out there. Those were painful recitals to watch (of course, I never told her that), but it never seemed to bother her outwardly. I think she thought she sounded fine. We were surprised that in the Merely Players production, she was loud and dramatic. It was great to see her blossoming.

Practicing for that production was how she met her future fiancé, Josh. Josh was the director of the bookstore on campus, and we knew from Erin that he was significantly older than she was—eighteen years older. We were a bit concerned about the age difference, but at the same time, Erin had always been an old soul, so we weren't that surprised by it, and my parents had a fourteen-year difference, so I was used to it. In the play, Josh played a retired famous actor on whom Erin had a major crush. Her character's fiancé, played by her friend Jon Bishop, had written a script that the retired actor played by Josh was going to star in. The first time we laid eyes on Josh, he was made up to look old, with white hair and wrinkles. We were hoping that it really was just makeup! We grew to love Josh greatly and still keep in touch with him today.

Erin made many lifetime friends in the theater group, including the group's faculty adviser, Professor Paul Shields, who always remained in contact with her. Paul was one of the last people to see Erin alive. He was the first person to send us flowers and a sympathy note after the accident. He told us that she was inseparable from his thoughts of Assumption. Erin was an integral part of the community and outdoor campus there.

Friends' Memories: Lauren Milka[13]

The following fall semester, Erin Sullivan convinced Erin to audition for a play she and I were producing— Tom Dudzick's "Don't Talk to the Actors." I will probably never forget Erin's audition. Having only had a few short albeit lovely conversations with Erin, I did not know much about her background with theater. But, after her audition, I knew Erin was right for the female lead. I am sure she was proud and probably nervous, but I will always be glad she agreed to act in the play, because it gave us the opportunity to bond and form our friendship over a mutual love for all things purple, Harrison Ford, Lord of the Rings, House, and cats. It's a little weird to look back on a play that happened almost four years ago and realize how much influence it had over the next few years. I had no idea Erin and Josh would start dating as a result of such a memorable scene between their characters, nor did I think that the play or theater in general would play such a central role in Erin's and my friendship.

Erin and Stephanie Plotkin.

Jon Bishop and Erin. Photo credit Stephanie Plotkin.

Used with permission of all models; public poster designed by Josh Moore (used with permission).

Erin's junior year just kept getting more exciting. In the spring, as part of her Central and Eastern European History course, she had the chance to visit some of the area, particularly Budapest, Vienna, Prague, and Bratislava. She got to know some of her classmates better and became close friends with one in particular, Danielle, whom she later asked to be her bridesmaid. The trip was amazing, and their photos attest to that.

Photo credit
Tracey Moretti.

Danielle Asdikian and
Erin. Photo credit Danielle
(Asdikian) Tsukuda.

After Erin returned from the trip, her friend from Idaho, fellow Lord of the Rings fan Anna Gorin, came to visit. While Anna was in town, she did a photo shoot of Erin and Josh and of Erin and her friend Chris. Anna graduated with an art degree and is a professional photographer. She takes amazing photos. If you go to her website, annagorin.com, you can see her gorgeous pictures. In fact, Erin's photo on the cover of this book is by Anna. In the last couple years, Anna has organized a hiking group, and she has taken breathtaking photos of the mountains in Idaho. I didn't realize the state was so picturesque. She and her friends have also taken photos in New Zealand (the filming areas for the Lord of the Rings movies especially) and Iceland. I digress. Anyway, Anna took many amazing photos, some of which we used as Erin's graduation pictures, and sadly but fortunately, we had them to use for Erin's wake and funeral displays and program.

It always amazed me how stylish Erin looked in whatever she wore. She certainly didn't inherit that from Abel or me! She was never a brand-name person and often shopped in thrift stores for her clothes in college. She was not a materialistic person.

Erin with Anna Gorin. Photo credits Anna Gorin.

Photo shoot. Top left: Erin with Josh. Photo credits Anna Gorin.

Photo credit Anna Gorin.

Photo credit Anna Gorin.

During the summer before her senior year, Erin took classes at the American Red Cross to become a certified nurse's aide and home health-care assistant. She did get her certificate and license, thinking she would be able to work during the school year at a nearby nursing home. As it turned out, they only hired experienced people, and the only places that hired inexperienced ones were not the best-quality homes. Josh, Abel, and I all thought she could take care of us in our old age, but that won't happen now. We're on our own—although I'm sure somehow, in some way we don't now understand, she will be sure we're taken care of.

Before Erin returned to school for her senior year, in August, the three of us squeezed in three nights at Pine Point Beach in Scarborough, Maine. We have always visited the ocean in Maine at least once in the summer since she was a baby, even if just to dip our feet in and give Erin a chance to use her paddleboard. The ocean air is so refreshing. My family lives in Maine, so we have taken many trips there over the years. Over the summer months, we had a couple opportunities for small family reunions. It was great to see some people we hadn't seen in years. For that brief visit to Pine Point, we got together with a small group of family for Erin's twenty-first birthday before she ran off to meet her college roommate, Erin Sullivan, in nearby Old Orchard Beach, Maine.

Speaking of family in Maine, Erin's great-aunt Anne died at the age of ninety on December 9, 2011. Anne's sister Catherine died also at the age of ninety on December 9, 2007. Then Erin died on December 9, sadly not at the age of ninety but at twenty-three, in 2013. Strange coincidence.

In the summer of 2011, Josh bought a farmhouse and barn in Spencer. It needed a lot of renovations. It was vacant when he bought it. There were mice, spiders, and other bugs in it. We knew Erin must have really loved Josh for her to live where spiders existed! She loved all animals and pretty much all living things, except spiders.

While Josh and his father worked on making the house more habitable, Josh and Erin lived with his parents nearby for those few months. During that time, Josh's parents and his grandmother, Nanny, who lived near his parents, got to know Erin better. They loved her as their own daughter and granddaughter.

Not long after they moved in, Erin and Josh adopted a cat from the local animal shelter—as a pet, of course, but with the added promise of eradicating their mice, I'm sure. They kept her name: Elainna. Elainna favored Josh, who was not a cat person but soon became one. The shelter thought she was three or four years old, but apparently, she was much older, because it wasn't long before she developed mature-cat problems. Fortunately, Elainna lived until March 4, 2017, so I imagine she was a great comfort and connection to Erin for Josh. A few months after Erin's death, Josh also adopted a dog, Connor, who was just a pup, as he and Erin had planned to get a dog. Not quite a year after Elainna's death, Josh adopted another cat, Sadie. What a beauty! She is a Siamese but without the typical Siamese personality. She is loving and affectionate to both Josh and Connor. We all feel that Erin had a part in placing them together.

Center: Josh and Erin, holding Elainna. Top left: Sadie. Top right: Elainna. Photo credit Anna Gorin. Bottom left: Sadie and Connor. Photo credit Josh Moore. Bottom right: Connor.

Sorry—I digress yet again. Big-time! Let's go back to college. During Erin's senior year (2011–2012), she presented her senior research project in visual anthropology and won first place. She wrote an ethnography (I had to look that one up!) on how fashion on college campuses influences which social groups students are drawn to. Her research involved visiting several local campuses in the Worcester area, interviewing students, taking photos of them, and having them sign consent forms for the study. I don't know where she came up with the idea, but it was creative. After she had presented her project, she left for a couple hours and returned later to pack up her display. Her poster with all the photos and information on it was missing. She never did find it, but she made a new friend in the provost's office, Michele, when she went there to inquire if anyone had brought her poster there. Michele hadn't seen it, but that interaction began a new relationship for them, which deepened when Erin ended up working in the same building as Michele after graduation.

So if you see a bootlegged research project for sale online, it could be Erin's!

The next two typed essays I found in Erin's belongings. I think they must have been for either a class or, more likely, Candlelight Prayer, an interdenominational prayer gathering at the college chapel. I've never been, but I believe a couple people would speak on a certain topic, and then there would be prayer and meditation with candles glowing in the darkness of the chapel.

Her first essay, which begins, "In April of this year …," mentions our illnesses during the spring and summer, so it must have been written in the fall of 2010, the beginning of her junior year, when she was twenty years old. The second piece, entitled "Hope," probably was written at that same time since she mentions acting, which she did in the fall of 2010. I just want to defend myself when Erin talks of the pressure as an only child to do well in college. That pressure must have come from within her because that's one thing we purposely avoided—we never applied pressure on her to excel in school. I feel sad that she felt that way and that I never knew it. I hope she was just being dramatic, as she often was. I especially love her advice in the last paragraph to look for those "small moments that God is quietly putting in your life to show you that He's there and to keep holding on" and her remark that "quiet prayer for me is what gave me the greatest hope. Speak to God, even if you don't think He's there, don't worry, He's just quietly listening."

I retyped both of her pages, as written, for better print clarity, as they had been folded several times.

Erin's first essay, probably written at the end of 2010, follows:

In April of this year, I was finally getting close to the end of my sophomore year at Assumption College. With finals on the horizon, you can know that I was already started [sic] to get stressed. Meanwhile I was facing a lot of troubles personally and becoming upset about problems going on in some of my most important relationships. My inner struggles started to make me question if God was really there for me. It was getting harder and harder to see that He was there around me and this made me feel more depressed as time went on. During the last week of April, my problems got worse. I received a call that my mom had been diagnosed with breast cancer. My mother was already a cancer survivor for 10 years but this did not help lessen the blow. I was devastated. All of a sudden my personal problems did not seem so bad at all but I was still wondering where God was through all this time. After hearing this news, I just wanted the semester to end so I could be at home with my family. I had already made plans for my summer and these plans involved me being away from home. I knew I had to give them up to stay at home but it was more important to me to be with my family. While I was at home taking care of my mother, I noticed my dad's health starting to decline. After much urging, my dad went to the doctors. The next day he had to have a triple bi-pass. The doctors said if he didn't have the surgery he would have died probably within the next few days. Now I had to turn my attention to both my parents. Both who I had almost lost. During this time I felt that it would have been the lowest point of my life but it wasn't. Something kept me going. Every day I had to drive into Boston to visit my dad while still taking care of my mom. During this time, instead of feeling alone, I was able to notice all the blessings around me. Both my parents made miracle recoveries and during this time we were all able to bond and become closer than we have ever been. Also, some of my greatest friends that I have ever had were there for me all the time. I will never forget them and I will cherish them always. Through this experience I was able to learn to look for God in little ways and notice how His blessings are all around you. Now whenever I reach a dark point in my life, I know to look around me and realize how He is always there.

Erin's second essay, also probably written at the end of 2010, follows:

Hope

When I was entering my first year here at Assumption College, you can imagine both the great fears and the excitement that I had. As great as freshman year was, I found myself still upset. I felt I truly wasn't being the person I was, I felt like I didn't have a lot of good friends and I wasn't doing as well as I was hoping for in most of my classes. I couldn't even decide on a major. My faith life was starting to lack and I felt guilty about it. I prayed to God every day to pull me from the depression that I felt hung over me but I felt like He was not listening. Being an only child, it was hard knowing that there was a lot of pressure on me to do well in college. From the outside things looked okay but on the inside I felt like my college experience was becoming a failure. I just still couldn't find where I fit in at Assumption.

Eventually after waiting and holding on to what little hope I did have, things worked out. My prayer life began to get stronger and I started noticing God quietly working in my life. In fact I noticed he had been working in my life the whole time but I just wasn't opening my eyes to it. My grades picked up and I finally decided on my major, Anthropology with minors in History and German. I started joining different groups on campus including Campus Ministry, working as the Photo Editor for Le Provocateur, and this semester, I even started doing something I used to love, acting. I ended up finding a wonderful group of friends. I have made some of the best friends in the world that I will ever have and I know these relationships will last for life. I was able to finally be myself and express myself the way I had always done before college and I felt loved and accepted. I felt like God was also finally close to me again, and that was the most important thing to me.

As hard as my college experience began, I continued to hope and God answered me. I have never been more happy than I am now with my school and the choices I have made, the people I know, and the groups I participate in. If you are ever having trouble hoping, look at the small moments that God is quietly putting in your life to show you that He's there and to keep holding on. Look for it in the high grade you might receive, the surprise phone call from your family or a close friend, the laughter you share when you hang out with your friends. I know that God definitely put those in my life. Especially giving me best friends here. Especially if it wasn't for one of my best friends here. We had been good friends since day one at school and have only grown closer since. I know God had put him in my life so soon in my college experience because he is one of the reasons that helped me continue on when times were tough. He is always there for me even during my darkest times and I know that that is God's way of showing me He's there bestowing me blessings to get me through this time of hope. And lastly, quiet prayer for me is what gave me the greatest hope. Speak to God, even if you don't think He's there, don't worry, He's just quietly listening. Things will get better and you will find that happiness in life.

Erin triumphantly graduated from Assumption in May 2012 earning her bachelor of arts degree with majors in anthropology and German and a minor in history. A week later, we had a big graduation party at the local country club to celebrate. It's odd when I think back. At the time, that whole day felt as if it were Josh and Erin's wedding reception to me. The hall was decorated as nicely as a wedding, and both sides of our family were there, as well as Josh's family. Josh and Erin greeted people and waved goodbye to them from the top of the wide, elegant staircase. I remember having to keep reminding myself that it was a graduation party, not a wedding. This was before they were even engaged, which didn't happen until August of the following year.

Josh and Erin at Assumption
College graduation, May 2012.

Erin and her parents at her graduation party.

Friends' Memories: Catie O'Flynn[14]

Erin was an amazing friend. She was always so caring in helping me to study, driving me places, memorizing lines and comforting me when things were stressful. She had such a calming presence and always made me smile and laugh. Erin was always so positive and no matter what was going on in her life she was always willing to help others … When we got to the event it was fun being around Erin as she was always dancing and so happy to be around friends. Also, during senior year when I came back early for training and there were not a lot of people on campus she visited me and took me out to dinner to keep me company. Even after we graduated from Assumption it was so great to see Erin practically every time I visited to see a Merely players show or musical.

Friends' Memories: Julianne Elouadih[15]

Freshman year [Erin's sophomore year]: A memory that really stands out with Erin from my freshman year, though, is when I was very sick, and she drove me to the hospital. She stayed there with me until after 3 a.m., and she even paid for my prescribed medication at CVS. When I tried to pay her back, I had to force her to take the money. That just reminds me of how Erin always did whatever she could for others without expecting anything in return.

Sophomore year [Erin's junior year]: A memory with Erin that especially stands out … was when she met me at the Midnight Breakfast the night of the fall semester's study day. It was on a Thursday night, and, while I wanted to be there, I was a little upset that I was missing the Chaplet of Divine Mercy at Adoration. I planned to go to Adoration afterwards, but I wouldn't be able to say the Chaplet because I didn't have it memorized. Erin told me that she would go to Adoration with me, then we could go somewhere else and pray the Chaplet together because she had it memorized. We went to Adoration, then we found an empty classroom in Kennedy where we prayed the Chaplet. Because of this, I was inspired to memorize the Chaplet over Christmas Break, and I try to say it every day. This is only one of the many examples of how Erin influenced me in my faith.

Senior year [Erin had already graduated the prior year but was then working in the graduate department]: During the beginning of the year, I was going through an extremely difficult time that I didn't talk to any of my friends about. I wish I had talked to Erin because I know she would have been there for me, but she unknowingly helped me through. I remember how we planned to hang out for only a few minutes one day after she got out of work so I could show her my room, but that turned into sitting in the lounge of my building for a couple hours just talking. I am extremely grateful for that memory because it reminds me of the way Erin and I could talk about anything, whether it was silly or serious. Having her as a friend helped me to get through many tough times even without her knowledge, and I am so thankful for that as well.

Friends' Memories: Katie Brodeur[16]
I can still remember the first time I ever met Erin. She was sitting at her desk in Nault hall going over her class schedule. A nervous freshman excited to begin a new adventure. I remember noting her Jonny [sic] Depp poster and guitar case and feeling grateful and relieved that I had finally met someone who I seemed to share commonalities with. I remember being nervous that I would not fit in with people in college because I wasn't into drinking or partying. I feel so lucky to have met Erin who was always willing to go to the mall or to target with me, or even just to walk around campus … She was always accepting of my weird quirks and even

was willing to follow me across a frozen bridge and stand outside the olive garden with me in the snow just to wait for a table so we could celebrate a friend's birthday.

I am appreciative that I had a friend like Erin who gave me permission to be myself. I am grateful that I never once had to pretend to be something I wasn't because she loved people for who they truly were. Transitioning to college life can be difficult and I was frequently home sick [sic]. Erin always understood that and never failed to be supportive and caring. She even listened to me recite my angst ridden poetry and was able to do so without laughing … Throughout all four years Erin was able to remind me to hold onto what was important … We must have had a billion inside jokes that I find myself laughing at from time to time. Erin had an infectious sense of humor that could brighten even the most difficult day. We were part of a tight crew that became more like a family. We took care of each other and celebrated each other's achievements. We talked about our futures and fantasized about a time when we would all be able to afford the luxuries like non collapsible furniture and food more substantial than easy mac.

Erin Sullivan, Chris Moran, and Erin. Photo credit Erin Sullivan.

Erin and Assumption College's president, Francesco Cesareo. Photo credit Erin Sullivan.

Erin with a new hairdo.
Photo credit Danielle
(Asdikian) Tsukuda.

Erin and Danielle
on the town. Photo
credit Mauricio
Tsukuda.

"The Look"—the closest Erin looked to being angry, per her roommate. Photo credit Erin Sullivan.

Erin with Chris Moran. Photo credit Erin Sullivan.

Crismel Calderon and Erin. Photo credit Crismel Calderon.

Erin with Catie O'Flynn.
Photo credit Catie O'Flynn.

Erin with her roommate, Erin
Sullivan. Photo credit Erin Sullivan.

Stephanie Giguere and Catie
O'Flynn. Photo credit Catie O'Flynn.

Erin with Julianne Elouadih.
Photo credit Joan Elouadih.

Erin with Siobhan
Bennett (Hazelwood)
and Erin Sullivan.

Erin with Erin Sullivan.

Chris Moran,
Erin, Katie
Brodeur
(Aston), and
Erin Sullivan.

Erin with Erin Sullivan.

Erin Sullivan, Erin,
and Chris Moran.

Photo credit Erin Sullivan.

CHAPTER 10

POSTCOLLEGE YEARS

About a week after the graduation party, Erin drove down to Baton Rouge, Louisiana, with her friend Chris Moran, who was moving there to work with Teach for America. She rode down with him and then flew back in time to begin her new job. Always the eager traveler, she had some nice photos of their various stops.

Erin's first official job after graduation was the position of administrative secretary in the graduate studies department at Assumption. She was told she had been chosen out of seventy applicants. There she developed many close long-term relationships among the faculty and staff of the school. In addition, she got to meet Josh every day for lunch. She worked there for a little more than a year.

Erin and Josh found time for a few trips. They enjoyed a trip to Vermont, where they stopped by to visit with Erin's old friend from the Connecticut Renaissance Faire: the sword swallower and hypnotist Roderick Russell, with whom she always kept in touch. Another trip to Bar Harbor, Maine, gave them a chance to relax and enjoy themselves for a few days before returning to do more work on their farmhouse.

In March 2013, Josh and Erin attended an anthropology conference in Washington, DC. They brought back many stories and photos chronicling that trip. Erin had enjoyed her classes at Assumption with Professor Amy Gazin-Schwartz, her cultural anthropology teacher and mentor, who helped Erin set up her special major and worked with her on her senior project. Amy also attended one or two of the same conferences Erin and Josh attended.

Erin played disc golf with Josh and his friends. Recently, in 2018, their friend Matt, when describing the way his daughter played disc golf on Facebook, said she played with "Erinesque Ease." When I asked him what that meant, he said, "[Erin] had a natural gift for throwing discs, and just about everything else. We marveled at her abilities."[17]

Erin and Josh.

Josh at the Lincoln Memorial.

Erin and Josh in Vermont.

Erin and Josh at the Rodriques family Christmas party.

Erin and Josh at the Morrisons' gathering.
Photo credit Leanne Morrison.

Erin was a major animal lover. Steve Irwin, the Crocodile Hunter, was her hero. She was devastated when he died in 2006. As I mentioned earlier, Erin and Josh had adopted a cat, Elainna, but they were also planning on eventually adopting a dog. She added bird feeders to the yard—which they found out isn't always a good idea when bears are in the area. One day they found a baby bird by itself in the yard, and of course, Erin tried to rescue it. She and Josh made a shoebox bed for it and kept it on top of the refrigerator overnight so Elainna could not get at it. In the morning, they drove almost an hour to bring the bird to a veterinary school of medicine hospital to see if they could help the bird. The staff signed the bird in and assured them they knew of someone who would adopt it. Erin would have had the house loaded with abandoned and sick animals if she could have—and Josh would have smiled and gone along with whatever she wanted.

I believe it was when Erin was working at Assumption that she decided to take a belly-dancing class to strengthen her core. Erin discovered the belly-dancing class sign when she was going to an appointment with her Lyme specialist one day. I laughingly said, "How can you do belly dancing? You don't have any belly to move around!" Another time, again jokingly, I said, "Couldn't you take tap dancing instead so I don't have to explain to Grammy that you're belly dancing?" I received the usual eye roll in response.

Once again, she made lifelong friends while belly dancing and enjoyed the classes. She even handmade one of her costumes for their folk dancing performance not far from our house at the annual New England Folk Festival (https://www.neffa.org). She was an elegant dancer. After hearing of Erin's death, the belly-dancing troupe posted a photo and heartfelt tribute for Erin on their website, www.evetribalbellydance.org. Click on the "Our Amazing Dancers" tab to see their beautiful "In Memoriam" post.

Abel, Erin, Kathy, and Josh at the New England Folk Festival.

Hannah Peterson and Erin.

Friends' Memories: Stephanie Giguere[18]

But my best memories of Erin come after graduation. We both worked at Assumption, and we would have lunch together almost every week. I looked forward to these lunches, where we shared much more than a meal; we told stories about our cats, shared concerns about our boyfriends, vented frustrations about our new adult lives, compared what we learned in our belly dancing classes, swapped new and old Assumption gossip, and laughed about pretty much everything.

I would share things with Erin that I wouldn't always share with other people, because I knew I would never feel judged, and often, she could relate. After lunch with Erin, I could return to face [the] difficult parts of my life with new perspective and strength because I knew I was not alone. I felt we shared a complex solidarity even in the simple phrase she often said to me; "I was thinking about you the other day."

After just a year, I stopped working at Assumption, and we didn't have regular lunch dates any more. We still met for dinner when we could. And one morning, at the very end of September, Erin and I had breakfast at the Miss Worcester diner. It was the perfect morning; the sun came in through the window onto our little booth, and the food was delicious. Erin had so much to tell me. She explained that she had quit her job and started working at the Bridge, and that she loved it there even though she wasn't making as much money as she did at Assumption. Then she told me that Josh had been laid off, but she was quick to assure me that this was a good thing, and that he was happy and hard at work turning his passion for design into a career. Things were getting done around the house—there was even a new bathroom door, she was proud to tell me. I had always admired Erin's beauty, but particularly on that day, as we walked out together and she showed me her new car, she emanated a profound sense of peace and joy.

Friends' Memories: Katie Brodeur[19]

As we continued to grow into adulthood our lives became more complicated but I never stopped enjoying my time with Erin. I can remember talking about music and guitar for hours, specifically the classic rock legends and the Grateful Dead. I would often find myself playing around on the guitar when we were all hanging out and Erin would stop mid-sentence and announce "I LOVE THAT SONG!!" Typically she and I would be the only two people in the room that had ever even heard the song before but it felt great to have someone to share the interest with. It is hard to find someone at age 23 who fully appreciates that kind of music but Erin was special and could enjoy the classics. I even got the opportunity to go to a Phish concert with her and Josh in Worcester. We all agreed that Phish put on a great show that night and were wowed by the playlist. It seemed like they were playing all our favorites just for us.

Friends' Memories: Anthony Rofino[20]
The last time I saw her. We did lunch at a Thai restaurant. Before that, we hadn't seen each other since our beach trip and we were both dying to hang out. It felt like no time had passed at all, as we filled the restaurant with laughter. Erin was so happy as she showed me her engagement ring and wedding dress and we talked about how our lives had been. I don't think we went more than a minute without laughing about something. It truly showed how happy and amazing she was and I had such a good time.

While Erin was working at Assumption, she applied and was accepted to their graduate school. She wanted to get her master's degree in rehabilitation counseling. I believe her idea at the time was to help returning soldiers and immigrants assimilate into society. She might have eventually chosen something else, but that was the last she told me. She had considered many careers throughout the years, including marine biology, nursing, occupational therapy, and environmental science. Most of these would have been difficult for her, as they included math, which did not come easily to her. She began taking graduate courses in rehab counseling in the summer of 2013.

An adviser in the counseling program suggested Erin find a job in the human services area so when it came time to do her clinical, she would be able to use those same work hours toward it. Two friends of hers, Allison and Amy, who worked at the Bridge of Central Massachusetts in Worcester and also were belly-dancing mates, told her about a job opening there that they thought Erin would be a good match for. Erin applied and was accepted as treatment coordinator for the Stepping Stones Program. She was assigned to that residence and began organizing, filing, and coordinating care once she got there. She was in the midst of taking classes to learn about supervising the administration of medications when *the* accident happened. She had become good friends with some of the staff, even going to basketball games, movies, and other activities with them. She enjoyed her job. Many of the staff traveled from Worcester to Mansfield to attend Erin's wake and funeral and were visibly upset—and they had only known her for three months. That was the big impact she had on them. She became a close friend and confidante quickly and easily.

Mini–college reunion at Cape Cod. Left to right: Erin, Erin Sullivan, Anthony Rofino, Katie Brodeur (Aston), and Lauren Milka. Photo credit Lauren Milka.

Lifeteen forever friends. Left to right: Patria Ferragamo, Erin, and Stephanie Storer. Photo credit Patria Ferragamo.

In early August of Erin's last year on this earth, Erin, Josh, Abel, and I took a meteor shower astronomy cruise out of Plymouth, Massachusetts,

Harbor. For me, it was one of the best experiences the four of us had shared. The boat left around nine o'clock at night, cruised out to the center of the bay, and sat there for a couple hours. We were on the inside first-floor section of the boat on the ride out. The engine was shut down, and as many lights as safely possible were turned off. When the boat settled in, our leader asked us all to go to the top deck. It was a surreal experience. I looked up as I climbed the stairs, and it seemed as if the Milky Way were the ceiling of the top deck—it looked that close! The narrator pointed to different planets and constellations with his laser, turning it off whenever planes were near. Since we were so far out, it was pitch black, with no city lights to dim the sky view. It was the first time in my life I had seen the Milky Way. Shooting stars were visible. It was as though we left Earth and its troubles for a while and were suspended outside of time. We arrived back at the dock around one in the morning. Erin and Josh stayed at our house and left for their home the following day. I have wonderful memories of that escapade. Should you want to have an amazing and unusual experience with your own family, I definitely suggest the same sky watching group, Mark's Tree Farm. The websites for their meteor cruises are http://www.astronomer-mark.com and http://www.meteorcruise.com. It's an outstanding family activity.

Before Erin left her job at Assumption and began her new position at the Bridge, she and Josh came with us to Maine for a few days during our vacation. We had an unplanned mini–family reunion while celebrating Erin's twenty-third birthday and her cousin Kevin's thirtieth birthday. Our goal was to have a picnic at Portland Head Light in Cape Elizabeth. It wasn't to be, I guess. It was the first time in my entire life that there was not a parking space available there, and we had about four cars in our entourage. Apparently, there was a boat race going on, as well as a wedding and probably some other events. We ended up eating in the picnic area outside Kevin's condo. It was the best time we had together in my memory. We laughed a lot, took photos, and told stories. It gave Josh some time to meet my side of the family.

None of us knew at the time that Josh had planned to propose to Erin at Portland Head Light that day, her actual birthday. What a disappointment it must have been for him when we couldn't find a place to park. The following day, Abel and I picked up my mother and joined Erin and Josh at a restaurant in South Portland for lunch. After we ate, as we were getting ready to leave, Josh wanted me to come take pictures of him and Erin on the dock. As I went around the corner with my camera, I heard my mother say, "What's happening? Did they drop something?" It appeared to her that Josh was bending down and looking on the dock for something. Confused, I looked at them, and Josh was kneeling down on one knee, holding Erin's hand in one hand and a ring in the other. Both of them were laughing and crying at the same time. Erin was totally surprised. Fortunately, we have the moment recorded in our photos. A bit rattled, Abel walked them to their car and, like any protective dad, made Josh promise to take care of his baby. Erin and Josh drove off to visit the Old Port in Portland and to call his parents to tell them the good news. The three of us left behind were still in shock, trying to figure out what had just happened. We were grateful Josh had chosen to propose while we were there to witness their profound moment.

Erin and Josh at Kevin's condo, August 17, 2013.

Josh proposes to Erin on the pier after lunch at the Saltwater
Grille in South Portland, Maine, August 18, 2013.

Over the next few months, we got together with Erin, Josh, and
his parents to check out the wedding venue. Erin set up their couple's
appointments for a marriage preparation class, and she and Josh met
with Father Greg for marriage discussions. Then I went with Erin to
look at wedding gowns. Her intention was not to buy one that day—just
to see what styles were available. However, she just knew that the second
dress she tried on was *the* dress. Abel was in the area and stopped by to
check on us. He went back out to the car for his camera and took more

than thirty pictures of Erin in her wedding gown and veil—complete with price tags on them. I know the groom is not supposed to see the dress until the wedding, but I'm pretty sure she texted Josh a photo! We at least had the pleasure of seeing Erin dressed as a bride.

Erin found her perfect gown at David's Bridal in North Attleboro, Massachusetts.

After David's Bridal, the three of us had dinner at the Emerald Square
Mall food court. This was the last photo Abel took of Erin.

On Saturday, December 7, two days before the accident, I met Erin
and her maid of honor, Erin Sullivan, her college roommate, to help
choose dresses for the two of us. Afterward, I gave them hugs goodbye,
and that was the last I ever saw of Erin.

Abel's last hug from Erin was at Thanksgiving. We were invited to
Josh's parents to gather with their extended family for Thanksgiving
dinner. We all excitedly talked about the upcoming wedding on May 31
and looked at the photos of Erin in her wedding dress. As it came time
to leave, Abel placed a Christmas wreath we had bought for Erin and
Josh in the trunk of her car. After giving hugs, away they drove.

Our new, painful, life-changing saga began.

PART 5

FROM ERIN'S PHYSICAL DEATH TO HER NEW LIFE

If it is His Will, we shall be together someday on this earth and
if it is not His Will for us to meet again on this earth
than [sic] we shall all definitely meet in the next life
and it will be the greatest thing to ever happen.
—Erin Rodriques, May 26, 2006 (fifteen years old)

Photo credit Prestige Portraits, used with permission.

Class of 2012
August 17, 1990–December 9, 2013

CHAPTER 11

GIFTS TO US

At the beginning of our grief therapy, our therapist, Barry, told us not to discount any extraordinary or unusual events that might occur. Other clients had related stories that were not usual happenings. I'm sure you've heard friends or others talk about supernatural things, such as a bulb that just happened to go on during a beloved's favorite song, a coin found in an unexpected place, or maybe just a feeling that loved ones are nearby.

Barry told us that Abel's first gift from Erin was that he was the person to find her. She wanted him to be the one. Maybe it was to help him through the guilt he felt for not being able to protect her 24-7. We don't know the reason. I remember that during the recovery, the kind police officer who was with us all night put his hand on Abel's shoulder and said, "I'm sorry. You shouldn't have had to be the one to find her. We should have found her." Of course, Abel doesn't remember because he was so out of it, but that is one of the few things from those days that stands out in my mind. So we'll take it as a gift from Erin that Abel was the one to find her.

Our next amazing gift came in March 2014, three months after the accident. We got a voice mail from a movie theater saying they had found Abel's wallet. Shocked, we recalled that we'd been with Erin the last time we had seen a movie at that theater, which was not far from where she lived. She always made sure she went with Abel to any new superhero movie, even if she had already seen it herself. That was one of their strong bonds: seeing superhero movies together. When he left the restroom after the movie that day, he discovered that his wallet, which had been in his back pocket, was missing. We didn't know if he had lost it or it had been stolen. He and Erin went back into the theater with the usher, who used his flashlight to look all around and under the seats. Nothing. Abel left his name and number at the service desk. We then looked all through the car to see if it had dropped out of his pocket there. Nothing. Off we went, going our separate ways. The more Abel thought about it, the more he was convinced he had probably dropped it while going into the gym the day before, next door to where he worked. He checked at the gym and looked all around the parking lot. Nothing. He filed a police report and then went through the grueling task of replacing everything in his wallet.

We received no word for the next several months. About eight months passed before we got the phone call. We thought they must have had the name and number confused. Our therapy session in Worcester just happened to be the next day, so we drove to the movie theater first, and Abel went in. When he told them about the phone message, the woman at the desk sent a young guy into the back to get the wallet. When he returned, he said there was no wallet there. The woman told him to go back again, as one of the staff had just found the wallet *yesterday*. This time, when he went back, it was right in front of him. The woman handed the wallet to Abel. He opened it, and Erin's graduation picture was staring at him. He cried, barely blurting out, "My daughter found it for me."

The woman said, "Wouldn't that make you happy that she found it?"

Then he told her about the accident. She and the others were familiar with it because it had been all over the newspapers and television out there. We were shocked that the wallet had just turned up eight months after he lost it and three months after Erin died. Of course, at therapy, Barry said it was the second gift Erin had given us.

When Abel called his mother that night, she said, "Did you tell Dennis yet? Call him, and tell him your story." So Abel called his brother Dennis and found out that on the morning of the accident, before anyone knew about the accident, Dennis had found on the top of his bureau a photo of Erin that he hadn't realized was there. The next day, after he found out about her death, he put the photo on the table next to his bed and set it up like a little shrine to Erin. Over the next couple months, he prayed for Erin and for us. Then he prayed to Erin, telling her that her father was having a hard time missing her, and asked her to try to do something to let him know she was okay. Then, after a while, he began to ask Erin to do something that only Abel would know about, so he'd know it had to be Erin. Specifically, he asked if she could find his wallet! It turned out that the photo he had found on his bureau and set up as a shrine on his bedside table was the exact photo staring out of Abel's wallet when he opened it at the movie theater. Believe what you want and any reason why this could have happened, but we're taking it as a gift from Erin to affirm to us that she is okay and watching over us.

In the months that followed that event, Erin's old college roommate, who was going to be her maid of honor, sent us copies of Facebook messages between the two of them, showing how concerned Erin had been about her father losing his wallet. She'd worried especially that the house key was in it, and she'd been afraid someone would break into the house. The more we read about her concern, the more we knew Erin must have been involved in finding the wallet. I don't pretend to understand how these things happen, but I'll take it!

Erin's graduation photo, the same one in Abel's wallet and on Dennis's table. Original photo credit Prestige Portraits, used with permission.

On February 3, 2015, my second birthday without Erin here to celebrate, Abel and I went to a local restaurant for my birthday dinner. One of the planets—Venus, I believe—was extremely bright that night over the lake. I felt it was a sign from Erin that she was with us. We kept saying she was probably sitting at the table with us throughout the meal. We were seated in the bar area, by a window overlooking the lake. Normally, we sit in the restaurant section, so that was an unfamiliar venue for us. When dinner was finished, the waitress brought over our bill. We took one look at it and nearly fell off our chairs. Take a look!

We must have looked so disturbed that the waitress came over to ask if everything was okay on the bill. We just said yes. I wanted to tell her how she had been part of our little Erin moment, but I was afraid I'd burst into tears. It was then that we noticed her name tag, which said, "Erin," in large letters. How did we ever miss that? Logically, she knew it was my birthday because I was using my birthday coupon for the meal. But think what you will—the pieces came together to make it a special message from Erin in our eyes. What makes us surer is that after we got the bill, Abel told me he had been outside in the cold by himself that afternoon, crying and begging Erin to do something special for Mom for her birthday if she could. Surely, this was the answer.

Other special moments included Josh, her fiancé, texting us well-wishes on birthdays, Mother's Day, Father's Day, Christmas, and other special days. I recently found a touching birthday card he must have given me on my first birthday without her, and my brain barely remembered it. We have kept in touch with Josh and his parents all these years. They are family to us.

Another friend of mine, Patricia,[21] told us a story of waiting in line with her daughter, Mary, outside the funeral home to get into Erin's wake in the subzero temperature. One of the people in line told Mary that she should bring up her van and let people take turns getting warm in it. Mary retrieved her van and parked next to the line, but no one wanted to get in; they were afraid they would miss some of the Erin stories people were exchanging. There was a pilgrimage feeling among them. At one point, Patricia saw a bunch of girls dancing around joyfully, and Patricia started judging them (in her words), thinking how disrespectful it was to be dancing at such a somber time. Standing in line next to her were my friends Jane and Arthur. They mentioned to Patricia that the girls were part of Erin's belly-dancing troupe and were honoring Erin with their dancing. Patricia said it was as if a lightbulb went off in her head: "Erin got it. All are welcome! God loves all of us; no one is excluded. Erin loved everyone too."

Soon after Patricia told us that story, we found a much older journal. Half-started journals are everywhere around the house, begun by Erin at all ages, even ones with only drawings before she could write. The one we found contained two special entries that Erin had written when she was ten years old. When I told Patricia the title of one of them, she said that it confirmed her lightbulb moment the night of the wake. The top of the page read, "All is welcome." The entries contained misspelled words and some incorrect grammar, but we got the point.

All is welcome.

by Erin Kate Rodriques

"All is welcome. Yes all is welcome." Say the Lord All can come to his house in ~~there~~ hevine. Oh yes all are welcome to his house.

To Day is the day

by erin Rodriques

To day is the Day that I shall
see the word face to face. I will
see the sea, I will sunrise and the
sunset, I will see the birds I will the
trees, I will stand on the shore,
And I will see the Lord stand
by me. "I say Amen to you" the
lord says. for I am the lord your
God Jesus Crist. He who
belives in me shall live forever.
And To Day is the day I shall
die and live And I shall rise on
The last Day. AMen"
Says the Lord!

4/12/01 on Holy Thursday. at 11:43
PM

Also, Patricia sent us a note that included the following:

> I didn't tell the story that night but that night I was recalling the time when Father Greg wanted to start a Charismatic Prayer Meeting and had us hold hands asking for the anointing of the Holy Spirit, I felt this heat from Erin's hand [Erin was about six] and the thought that went through my mind was, "I think Erin is the only one that got it." It was a similar experience to being aware that Erin got it, the night of Erin's wake. I had shared that with you at a later time. God Bless. Erin's impact on this world was and is extraordinary.

Another gift for Patricia is that she has been asking for Erin's intercession for a serious health issue of a member of her family. A couple signs have happened concerning his improvement, and she will be monitoring his continued progress and keeping us posted.

I unexpectedly found another journal of Erin's on Saturday morning, March 4, 2017. Abel was staying overnight with his mother, as she had been seriously ill, and when I'm alone in the house, I can't sleep, so I was up most of the night. Late the next morning, I was at the bedroom window, looking out at the spring sky, and as I turned around, my eyes landed on a journal next to a space on the shelf where I had removed my own journal I had started years ago shortly after Erin was born, in which I'd written significant things in it for her to read after I died. I also had some of my favorite books on that shelf to leave for her. After Erin died, I took down my own journal and started writing about things since her death. I was surprised to see a journal next to that empty space where mine once was. I thought to myself, *I don't remember starting a second journal. Why would I do that if I haven't even finished the first one?* Well, it wasn't mine; it was Erin's. She had started it on March 14, 2004, when she was just thirteen years old. How could we not have noticed it for thirteen years? It was right there in plain sight! Abel had just searched those shelves in the previous two weeks, looking for donations to charity, and he's always got his sharp eyes peeled for anything of Erin's.

When I started reading the journal, I burst out sobbing. It began as a normal journal, and then there were two letters to us—a "Dear Mom" and a "Dear Dad" letter. As I read them, I was taken aback. I couldn't figure out why she had written them as though she had already died. It was a strange feeling, as though she had just written them the day before and placed the journal on the shelf for us to find. For the prior two weeks, I had been wondering if Erin still loved me in her independence at twenty-three as much as she had loved me when she was younger. I'm also always saying how much I miss her hugs and her laughter. Her love for me and her laughter are both mentioned in her letter to me. I was reading her words almost exactly thirteen years later to the day, and she was telling me about the sun shining on a spring day just like the one I was experiencing at that moment.

I have inserted some of the pages from that journal after this section. After much thought, I believe I might have told Erin about the journal I was making for her, and maybe she got the idea to make one herself for anyone she was leaving behind, should she die first. At the end of the book, she wrote a long list with three columns of all the people she was praying for, including friends, family, movie stars, and musicians. At the top of each page, she had prewritten, "Dear Liz," "Dear Grammy," and so on. She ended up actually completing only a few of them. Luckily, she had finished the ones for Abel and me. If my own journal was not her reason for writing them the way she did, maybe it was an assignment or suggestion at a retreat. A friend told me not to try to rationalize it but to just take it as a gift from God that I found the journal when I did. I definitely needed to see it.

Since Erin wrote that she started the journal on March 14, 2004, I would say that the individual letters were written somewhere between then and early 2008. The letter to me is the first of the individual letters, and she mentions her first time at Steubenville East, which was the summer after eighth grade, in 2004. However, some of the people she wrote to were not known to her until a year or so later.

It was sad but comforting that Erin seemed not to be upset about her demise. It was just a normal next step to her. She seemed perfectly content with it in her letters. I have to believe that she is waiting for us to be with her face to face once more. Until then, I know she is with us spiritually. There are too many Erin incidents to deny it. As I looked back on that weekend when I found the journal, I noted how many significant events happened all together. Friday, the day before, Abel and I had spent the day with Josh's parents, going out to lunch and then to a travel exposition. That night, as I said, I was alone while Abel was with his sick mother, Erin's grandmother. Saturday, the next morning, I found Erin's significant letters, and the following day, Josh got in touch with us about Elainna, their beloved cat, who'd died the night before, the same day I found the journal. The front of the journal was decorated with butterflies, symbols of new life, and hydrangeas—with much purple and blue, Erin's favorite colors—which are reminders of her memorial garden. Everything seemed to come together in a little packaged gift of comfort.

"Therefore if any man be in Christ, he is a new creature." II Corinthians 5:17

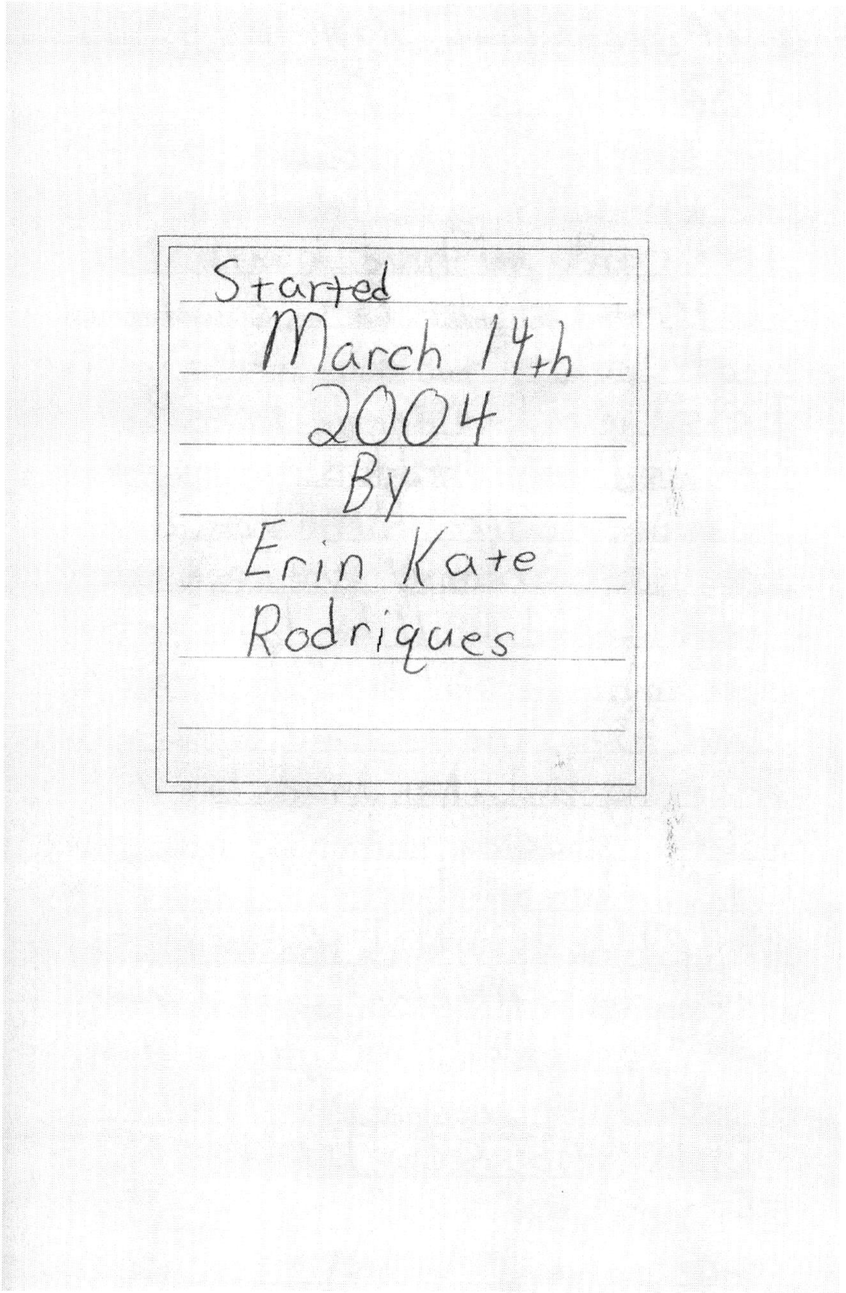

Started
March 14th
2004
By
Erin Kate
Rodriques

✺ March 14th, 2004 12:32 AM

HI! Today is my first time writing in this book. I'm sorry if the writing is bad. I am very tired and my hand hurts. I am listening to the PotC soundtrack right now. It just went to track 2. I want to audition for the next PotC movie. It says I need headshots and an agent. I have neither. Headshots are too much money and a good agent and would be hard to find in a small town like Norton. Today at 4:30pm I have an EDGE meeting and then mass at 6. EDGE is going to be speicial today. It is the St. Patrick's Day Party! Well, I'm afiad I have to stop writing now. My mom said I need my rest. It's 12:38 AM. I'll probably write more soon. The PotC CD is on track 5. But I need to turn it off now.

    Love,

      ~~Erin~~ Erin Kate

April 12th, 2004 11:29pm
Hi! I'm so sorry that I haven't written. I have been so busy. Anyway, St. Pat's Party was a blast! On Good Friday we went to Patriots Cinema to go see Master + Commander but when we got there, the times had changed. So we so Peter Pan. I guess it was good. Just you've seen one Peter Pan movie, you've seen them all. God probably punished us with that for going to the theater on Good Friday. After that we went to ME. On Sat. I decorated the church with Grammy. I put the plants everywhere and I helped a guy named Joe, put the water in the tub. On Sunday we had dinner. It was at Grammy's! Then later on we saw the Passion. I didn't cry! There must be something wrong with me! I sobbed so much when I saw it the first time. Then today we came HOME! I have to go to bed now! Goodnight! Love, Erin Kate

165

Dear Mom,
On the night of my very first time at Steubenville, Marie, Kim Possible and I were talking about our relationships with our moms and when I was asked about mine, I told them that I had the best one anyone could ever ask for. I love you so much! I'm so sorry for all the times I made fun of you and said you were stupid, crazy and uncool. You were really as cool as cool could be! I would never trade you in for all the riches in the world. You are the best mom ever, and I'll miss you so much untill we see each other again! All the times I spent with you were the best times of my life! I'll still be missing you + praying for you! Anytime the sun shines on a springday, know that it's me smiling + laughing. :)
Love you!!! Love from your daughter,
            Erin Kate Rodriques

Dear Dad,

First I want you to know how sorry I am that I have yelled at you and treated you badly alot. It's hard to say but, it was like the more I did, the more I loved you. They say that the people who act like they can't stand each other are the ones that love each other the most. You were the best dad anyone could ever ask for. I'll always remember the great times we had together. I can't wait for the day that we see each other again and all the wonderful times we'll have together again. I'll be missing you alot and will always be thinking of you. Thank you from the bottom of my heart for always being there for me and for always being my Dad. :)
I love you so much!!!

Love forever,
Your daughter Erin Kate Rodriques

Dear Alex,

Alex! Gosh, what can I say about a guy like you? You are so one of the coolest guys I have ever met. I'll always remember how hard you could make me laugh.

Thanks for all the good times and thank you so much for being such a great friend. I can't wait till we meet again! I'm going to miss you sooo much !!! I hope that everything turns out great for you and that you have The Time Of Your Life.

Remember that time is a precious thing so don't be afraid to tell someone you love them or if you just want to dance randomly in the streets! :) ! I miss ya!

With love,
Erin

Dear Bernie,

Hi Bernie! I first have got to tell you that one of the biggest blessings ever was to know you. You are such an awesome man of God! You also always would bring joy to me. I'd feel so at peace every time you would sing "It covers me" and "Misting Over Me" You have one of the most beautiful and pure voices I have ever heard. I hope that you continue to light the world with God's love. I'm going to miss you so much and I can't wait till I get to see you again! Please always remember me, I'll always remember you. And know that anytime you are playing or singing, I'm looking down and dancing along. :

With great love,
Erin

In the summer of 2017, while Abel was in Erin's room, he found a box of old audio cassettes Erin had recorded. What a find—or maybe another gift from Erin. Some were recorded secretly with a friend when she was probably only around seven or so. Erin and her friend recorded Abel and me while we were totally unaware. There were some of her reading or pretending to read, practicing repeatedly from the beginning. My favorite was a cassette on which she describes the first couple days in Germany for World Youth Day as she was turning fifteen. I was hesitant at first to listen to it, as I thought it would be emotionally unbearable to hear her voice. I'm glad I decided to listen to it. After I listened to her, it was as though she had been sitting next to me on the couch, excitedly telling me every detail of our trip. What a great gift it was to find those tapes! These little Erin moments always seem to come at just the right time. Our new friend in media at Assumption, Laurie Palumbo, graciously made digital recordings of them for us so they would be preserved longer.

Many other Erin events have happened to us and to her family and friends, who still experience a close bond with Erin. Some of them I will share more about on my website (see the appendix). In this book, I would rather have you focus on Erin's actual writings to interpret in your own way and, hopefully, establish your own bond with her.

CHAPTER 12

MEMORIALS AND TRIBUTES TO ERIN

Memorials and tributes to Erin began the day we found Erin's overturned car. Friends and the president of Assumption College were quoted in various news reports speaking of a joy-filled, kind, compassionate, and genuine person who was beautiful inside and out. Her graduate course instructor at that time canceled his final that night because the campus and the students in her class were all distraught. The flag was flown at half-mast for her. On that Friday after the accident, a memorial prayer vigil at Assumption was attended by her friends, work colleagues, teachers, clergy, and fellow students. The following comments by Erin's friend, Crismel Calderon, were included in the program for the prayer vigil,[22]

> For as little as I knew her (only through senior year), I grew very close to her and trusted her with details and secrets I could never share with my closest friends. I care so much for her and think of her often but it gives me peace, as it should to you as well, that Erin lived a life that anyone would be envious of. She was sweet, smart, caring, funny and genuine. And to touch as many lives as she did, including mine very deeply, in only 23 years is nothing short of awe inspiring.

An article followed in *Le Provocateur*, her beloved college newspaper, about Erin's life at Assumption and after, complete with photos of her smiling face.

When I asked Tim Stanton, the vice president for Institutional Advancement at Assumption, if we could have a tree and memorial plaque for Erin, he said that Cindy Washbourne, a work colleague and friend of Erin, had already inquired about creating a memorial garden for her. Several fellow staff members were interested in the project. With the assistance of Todd Derderian, the head of Building and Grounds at the time, and after much preparation and hard work, Bouba Coulibaly from the landscaping crew commenced with the project, and where a tangled mess of bushes and many rocks of all sizes once stood, a gorgeous garden grows today. Bouba and Cindy both knew Erin, so the process was a gift of love for them. Abel and Erin's friends and family have added many more plants to the garden, and we visit at least a couple times a month to care for it. Abel lovingly does the hard work while I talk to people stopping to visit.

Erin's Memorial Garden has been a miracle for staff and students. It is a haven of peace in which people can gather their thoughts, including those who didn't even know Erin. Occasionally, I will hear a story or see a Facebook post about someone visiting the Garden. Laurie Palumbo from the media department visits it often and has gifted us with many photos of the Garden in bloom as well as shots of hummingbirds and butterflies enjoying its beauty. Beth in the IT department refilled the hummingbird feeders for us when we couldn't get there. We found out that Janet, who is now in the nursing department, has been refilling the suet in the birdfeeders all winter, even in knee-deep snow. John, Cindy, Laurie, and Christine watered during those early years, and I know there must be anonymous visitors who pull weeds too.

While the Garden was being created, Abel and I used to stop at the college almost weekly after our therapy with Barry to check on the Garden and have lunch with some of Erin's work colleagues, especially Cindy Washbourne, Susan Sabelli, and the late Christine Estabrook, who didn't know Erin personally but got to know her through our visits. While we ate in the dining hall, other friends, teachers, and colleagues of Erin would stop by for a chat too, especially Bob Bureau, Lee Pearson,

Paul Shields, Mike Land, and John Landers. We received great comfort from all of them in the place where we knew Erin had spent much of her time. They all are dear to us.

As an aside, in the spring of 2016, a year before Christine died, she drew an amazing portrait of Erin from a photo taken by Anna Gorin. When we first opened Christine's gift, I gasped—it was so lifelike. It looked as if Erin herself were staring up at me. What a treasure! There's a little bit of emptiness in the Garden without Christine's visits. We hope she and Erin have finally met each other.

Artist credit Christine Estabrook, used with permission.

Original photo that Christine used to draw Erin's portrait.
Photo credit Anna Gorin, used with permission.

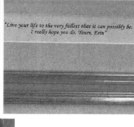

Erin's journal entry that Christine added to the framed drawing: 'Live your life to the very fullest that it can possibly be. I really hope you do. Yours, Erin.'

Christine Estabrook holding her drawing of Erin.

All of the hard labor in creating the Garden that summer of 2014 led to a Mass and Garden Dedication in September. Many friends, family, and work colleagues gathered with us to celebrate Erin's life. Father Vo Tran Gia Dinh celebrated the Mass with Brother (now Father) Ron Sibugan assisting. They both knew Erin well. In his homily, Father Dinh read from Erin's journals with tears streaming down his face. After the Mass, we all processed up to the Garden. Charlie, Mary-Jo's husband, thankfully, was photographing the Garden while Assumption recorded a video of the speakers at the dedication.

At Erin's Garden, President Cesareo and Father Dinh gave uplifting and hopeful talks about Erin, bringing smiles and laughter to those in attendance. I remember Father Dinh saying that if we want to see Erin, we must go to God in prayer, and we will meet Erin, because if Erin is with God, we'll meet her too. Father Dinh also remembered a time when their group was meeting after a 9/11 memorial one year, and they were offering prayers for family and friends. Erin asked if he would offer Mass for Osama bin Laden because nobody was probably praying for him. He was moved by her request, which reflected a true Christian virtue: loving and praying for your enemies. Her heart was so big that it encompassed not only her friends but also her enemies. Father Dinh said that through all of Erin's spiritual ups and downs, she never lost hope and that was so amazing to him. He was able to walk with her in her spiritual life for a short time. She "trusted [God], trusted, and trusted"—an amazing grace that we all need. Father Dinh reminded us that as we pass by her memorial Garden, "she will be here and she will smile at us and give us the light of hope as she did her entire life."[23]

I will summarize President Cesareo's many beautiful remarks about Erin. He first said that the "Garden is a reflection of who Erin was." The garden area used to be the least attractive part of the campus landscaping. When he heard that was the place where Erin's Garden would be, he thought it was appropriate not only because it was located behind the grad school building but also because Erin herself brought beauty to the "world and to the campus because of her own inner beauty that shone through her eyes, through her smile, and through her gentle spirit." President Cesareo came to know her better when she joined the college's *In the Footsteps of Father D'Alzon* Pilgrimage to Rome and

Paris. He "recognized her quiet spirit but the strength of her soul." He said that Erin was a young woman who saw beauty in everything—that's why she took so many photographs. Everywhere they went she always had her camera ready to go, constantly throughout the trip, he joked. She saw the face of God in everything around her. Erin herself "reflected the image and love of God." "That's what made her so special and gave her strength." She herself reflected the face of God because she saw it in all the beauty around her. "The Garden is a reflection not only of who Erin was but more importantly of the beauty of God's creation that she was enamored with; that filled her soul, that filled her spirit, that filled her life." The Garden helps us not only to recall her but to recognize that Erin is with us in a new way now. "She is now in the presence of the One to whom she loved and gave meaning to all she did." "The Garden reminds us that Erin is still with us, still reminding us, still prodding us," as Erin was known to nudge people a little bit further. Each time we pass by the Garden, he advised us to recall her life, and her continued presence in our hearts and memories. He said that the Garden reminds us that Erin is still with us because she is with God. President Cesareo addressed Abel and me, and our extended family and friends, reminding us to always feel that we have a special place on campus because of this beautiful Garden. He asked "her friends who pass by, in the years to come, to keep alive her spirit, her love, her embrace." He finished by saying that he knows the first question Abel and I will want to ask when it's our turn to meet God: "Why did you do this?" and Erin will probably answer for God! [But we'll be so happy to see her that we won't even care about the reason.] President Cesareo reminded our family and friends that we are not alone in missing Erin. The entire Assumption community was touched by her each and every day.

President Cesareo announced the establishment of Erin's Book Fund for those who wanted to donate to Assumption in Erin's memory. The new book fund will be used to purchase books for social rehabilitation students who otherwise might not be able to afford the books. This was another way "of Erin continuing her life, her legacy here on this campus." [24] [It also honored Josh, who had been the manager of the college's bookstore.]

Others gave testimonials of Erin. We did as well. I read several of the enclosed passages from Erin's journals and gave thanks to all who'd been involved in creating the garden, with special thanks to Bouba Coulibaly for his love and care in helping to create and design Erin's Garden.

Father Barry Bercier told us that Erin was a "theology teacher's dream." She was one of the few students who would have chosen to take his class even if it weren't mandatory. She "wanted to know about God and the mystery of life." He said that Erin sat in the front row, deeply engaged in the course he taught. Father Barry also mentioned her journal entry about her longing for eternity. We all have that longing for eternity deep in our hearts, but few can articulate it or even identify it. That was why she was eager to listen and intent on learning something from him. He said that sometimes students come along who surpass him and other theology teachers, and Erin was one of those students. Regarding eternity, "she has surpassed the whole bunch of us."[25]

Her friend and college roommate, Erin Sullivan, said that even when Erin lived off campus, she still was always there, taking photos for the *Provoc* or just personal use. She hung out at Charley's with Erin S., Chris, and the gang. Of course, she was also on campus for the Merely Players practice and performances, through which she'd met Josh. Erin Sullivan told the crowd that Erin would have been embarrassed by all this; she didn't like to be the center of attention and didn't like people to make a fuss about her. Erin would have been embarrassed for herself, but she would have been happy the Garden and Memorial were done for the people who were here missing her.[26]

I have paraphrased Elisabeth Solbakken's words. Erin's especially beloved German teacher recalled her lovely presence and said it had been a joy to see Erin mature during the four years she'd had Erin in her German classes. What impressed her about Erin as a person was her kindness. Elisabeth remembered looking out the window several times in the fall and seeing Erin take bewildered freshmen under her wing and help them find their way around. "Her kindness to others was always felt." What impressed Elisabeth about "Erin as a student was her incredible academic curiosity, a passion for learning"—a trait she's sure other professors who had Erin would fully recognize. She said, "Erin wanted to learn German after her trip to World Youth

Day in Cologne during high school, and she certainly did." Elisabeth finished by reading "Wandrers Nachtlied," a German poem by Johann Wolfgang von Goethe, for Erin. She said only Erin would have been able to translate, and she would have given a very beautiful interpretation of it.[27] Erin loved Elisabeth's classes, especially the German cultural ones, wherein they cooked German food, sang German songs, and read and discussed a variety of German literature.

Lee Pearson was a teacher Erin had at the time of the accident. Lee had also worked with Erin at Assumption during that last year. He had been thrilled when he found out that Erin had applied for their graduate school. His class was part of her rehabilitation counseling graduate program. Lee said that Erin was unique in many ways. He too said Erin always sat in the usually vacant front-row center seat for every single class, and added that Erin "was an outstanding student and a beautiful person. It was a pleasure to have known her."[28]

Michele Aubin from the provost's office, who "had the privilege" of working downstairs from Erin that year, recalled the story that I previously mentioned of the occasion of her first meeting Erin. Prior to their working together, when Erin was a senior, she went to Michele's office to see if her winning symposium poster had been brought there, because it was missing. Erin came back often to check to see if had been returned there. It was customary for Michele to photograph the winners and place the photos with their certificates in the display case near her office. When Michele took Erin's picture, Michele said she was thinking of how beautiful Erin was, and Erin looked at it and said, "Oh my gosh, I look terrible!" Once again, she was embarrassed to have any special recognition. Erin couldn't wait for the following year's symposium so the new winners' photos would replace her photo in the display case. Michele and Erin became closer throughout the year Erin worked there after graduation. Michele said that Erin was the "whole package." She had brains and beauty, especially her inner beauty. Michele felt that the book fund created and the Garden combined the two beautifully.[29]

Arthur Siegel, a personal longtime friend of ours and fellow colleague of mine when I was still working at McLean Hospital, didn't want to leave out Erin's love for pets. Animals were a big part of Erin's life. He recalled when her first pet, a hamster she loved, died; Erin was so upset that we had to memorialize the hamster with a funeral complete with songs and prayers. The shirt Arthur was wearing, given to him by his wife, Jane, bore the command "Be the person your dog thinks you are." He said we can put Erin, instead of "your dog," in that saying. "That's how she lifted us up. We can all continue to be the person Erin thinks we are."[30]

Mike Land, as I previously mentioned, was the adviser for the school newspaper, *Le Provocateur*. He believed that Erin was the first photo editor of the paper, and in that role, she greatly enhanced the paper with her photos. Mike also loves photography. They always ended up in the same places at different times, taking the same shots, notably on the Wachuset Meadow Trail or around campus. He talked about Erin's "keen artistic eye." He was so used to meeting up with her and seeing her around that he has to keep reminding himself that they never actually had class together. Erin was a good friend who, in addition to their photography, also came to readings, and he remembered the time he, Erin, and Erin Sullivan suffered through a long line to get the autograph of David Sedaris. Even today, when he is roaming about looking for photo subjects, he wonders what Erin would do with the same scene.[31]

Paul Shields, as I also previously mentioned, from the English department, was the faculty adviser for the Merely Players acting group, of which Erin was a member for much of her time at Assumption. He said that Erin is missed profoundly, and it was great to get to know her through that program. He said Erin is inseparable from his experience of Assumption as a whole. He was used to seeing her in many places on campus. It will not just be the Garden to remind him of Erin.[32]

Her friend and schoolmate Anthony Rofino described Erin as "so awesome" and said she "had so many friends." He wanted to share an experience of that day with the rest of the gathering. He said that during the homily at the dedication Mass, he was feeling sad, thinking about Erin, and as his eyes looked down at the hymnal, a purple light shone on the book. Purple was Erin's favorite color—that was why he was wearing a purple shirt. He felt that the sign of the purple light was Erin telling him, "Be happy that we're having this moment together. I'm all right." He wanted others to know her message too.[33]

Josh's father, Terry, spoke for the family. He is a private person, so

I will not quote him here. He did say that Josh loved Erin very much, and so did they. They wished they could have gotten to know her even more. He also thanked Abel and me for having her.

Susan Sabelli of the human services graduate program, who knew Erin from her work days as well as her graduate school days, said that Erin extended herself to everybody. Suitably, after Josh's father's words, Susan told of Erin's great love for Josh. Every time Susan walks into the dining hall and looks at the tables and chairs by the windows, she can't help but picture Josh and Erin there, even today. She vividly remembers Erin and Josh having lunch there every day for the year Erin worked at Assumption. Susan said that others left them alone; no one ever intruded upon their space. Erin had a special love for Josh.[34]

It was a wonderful and comforting day. On our way home, as Abel and I drove down the highway, I happened to glance out the window up at the sky, and my eyes landed directly on an unusual prism—not a rainbow but a short, beautiful prism. There might be a scientific explanation for it, but I gladly took it as a sign from Erin that all was well. It was a fitting closing confirmation for an amazing Erin day.

In December, after the dedication, I received a private Facebook message from a junior, Molly Sweeney, who hadn't known Erin but had heard about her. She wanted to let me know about something she'd experienced on her way to a function (I found out much later that it was a Merely Players performance) in "the pouring rain":

> I saw the Christmas lights on the tree and it was truly light in the darkness of the night. It brought light to a night that was otherwise lacking brightness and I know it was Erin's spirit shining down on the Assumption Community.[35]

Then, on March 19, 2016, the feast of St. Joseph, she sent the following photo, captioned, "Erin is shining down at assumption today!" Molly didn't notice the rays of light until after she took the photo. The rays reminded me of the rays of love and mercy seen in *The Divine Mercy* painting. By the way, Molly was on the *Provoc* staff too, as was Erin.

Photo credit Molly Sweeney, with permission.

As you can gather, Erin's Memorial Garden is probably the most significant memorial for her as well as for her friends and family.

Erin's Memorial Garden at Assumption College, Worcester, Massachusetts.

Erin's Memorial Garden holds many gifts from her friends and family. Hummingbird and butterfly photo credits Laurie Palumbo, used with permission.

More than a handful of people have told us they currently read Erin's writings as their meditations or when they need a boost. One deacon and several priests have used them in their homilies. Deacon Paul Kline[36] read one of her writings in particular at his college presentation to mental health clinicians working in Boston. The presentation explored spiritual pathways to living with mental illness. One part of his presentation explored the spiritual suffering of despair and hopelessness. He shared the story of our family and our terrible loss. He also "shared with them the wisdom that Erin left in the journal she kept as a teenager." The passage he read was the following:

> You know, sometimes this world seems like a dark and empty place and you can see some of the worst things in it and eventually it looks completely hopeless and you feel so alone in a world of sin and doubt. But, then you search and you find little scraps of hope and you continue to hold on to them and eventually you see the world in a most beautiful light and you are so full of hope and you find reasons to live, reasons to go on.

A few people, including Deacon Paul, referred to Erin as a modern-day prophet. I'm not sure what they mean by that—maybe her writings and actions conveyed messages of how God loves us and wants us to live. She definitely was specially anointed by God to bring His mercy, love, and light to others through her way of life for this dark world, and I can't wait to see her and discuss it all with her in the next life.

In addition to her Memorial Garden at Assumption, we also have a beautiful and meaningful monument at the cemetery where Erin is buried. I hadn't even known the cemetery existed before we had the unfortunate need to use it. Now Abel and I are set up with plots and a memorial stone for our turns. We ordered a black stone monument and had Erin's photo of Portland Head Light added to the front. In addition, we have a ceramic photo of Erin on the front left. To the right of the photo is the inscription "I will see you again and your hearts will be full of joy" (an interpretation of part of John 16:22 from the St. Joseph's edition of the New American Bible), and the bottom of the front reads,

"Love never ends." On the back of the stone, we have a ceramic photo of the three of us and another of Erin alone. Abel is busy keeping that garden beautiful and inspiring as well.

Erin's monument in Timothy Plain Cemetery, Norton, Massachusetts.

One event that deeply touched us five months after the funeral, days before her and Josh's wedding was to happen, was visiting her grave site and discovering a shoebox decorated with Erin's name and filled with letters, along with flower bouquets and a single red rose without thorns. After some sleuthing, we found that a group of clients and staff had come down from Stepping Stones, where Erin was working at the time of her death, and performed a memorial service of their own at

Erin's grave. I was told they had said a prayer and read from Erin's journal, paying their respects to her. We were moved by this kind and touching act.

One more recent memorial is a plaque added to the memorial bench for Abel's mother at the LaSalette Shrine in Attleboro, Massachusetts. Now the bench has two plaques on it: one for Abel's mother and one for Erin. Of course, Abel has planted yet another garden around it. It is probably the most perfect location for the memorial bench on the shrine grounds. We wanted the plaque and bench to be sources of solace and inspiration for people walking by or sitting in that spot, so we added one of Erin's quotes, written when she was fifteen years old: "NEVER lose hope! God is always there for you and He will never leave your side."

Many of Erin's friends and family have created their own memorials to her in the form of photo magnets, donations to charities that Erin admired or contributed to, wall collages, photos on dashboards, garden decorations, plants, and a photo book with friends' testimonials. We've also been told stories of Erin continuing to guide and inspire her friends and family. One of Erin's friends shared a cute story of Erin in college. The students were collecting items for the nearby Pregnancy Resource Center. Instead of or in addition to the usual baby items, Erin would donate some pampering things, such as Bath and Body Works shampoo and lotions, for the mothers-to-be. Erin had a huge heart and was always thinking of other people's needs.

Josh's creative works of art at Rockers Ranch on Etsy, inspired by Erin. Photo credit Josh Moore, with permission.

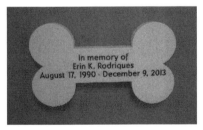

In memory of
Erin K. Rodriques
August 17, 1990 - December 9, 2013

Erin's friend saw this donation plaque in Erin's name on the wall of an animal shelter. Everyone knew of Erin's great love for animals. Photo credit Leanne Morrison, with permission.

Lockets with Erin's photo and locks of hair for Mom, Grammy, and VoVo.

Vigil for Erin in the Chapel of the Holy Spirit at Assumption College in the days after the accident. Photo credit Stephanie McCaffrey.

Memorial "leaves" at LaSalette Shrine, Attleboro, Massachusetts.

On Danielle's dashboard. Photo credit Danielle (Asdikian) Tsukuda, used with permission.

Commemorative Christmas
decorations made by Erin's parents
and family. Top left is created by her
Aunt Brenda, using cloth remnants
from costumes Erin had made.

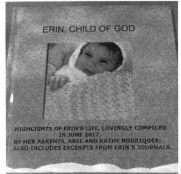

Erin, Child of God, a short book
of Erin's life in photos with
some of her writings included,
written by her parents

Collage of Facebook pictures
compiled by Erin's cousin Robbi
Coite. Used with permission.

Erin Kate Rodriques, a book compiled by Katie Brodeur (Aston) and friends of Erin, featuring friends' memories of Erin and photos. Used with permission.

Facebook heart of Erin's photos made by her cousin Ashley Vargas. Used with permission.

Drawing of Erin by our friend Lou Cappiello. Used with his permission.

Friends' Memories: Katie Brodeur[37]

When you move away from home you look for support. You're no longer surrounded by your parents and siblings and the idea of eating dinner in a dining hall by yourself is terrifying. I will always be grateful that because of Erin and the rest of our group, I never had to eat alone. Before we left Assumption I remember discussing my anxieties with Erin. I was worried that once we left Assumption we would grow apart and lose touch. Although this did happen with many people I had become close with at school, my relationship with Erin remained strong. I believe that this is the mark of a true friendship. Time and distance do not affect your love for the person. I was thrilled to hear of Erin's engagement and her new job. I was impressed to learn that she would be pursuing a master's degree and was always amazed at how she was able to carry herself with a quiet and humble nature despite the fact that she had accomplished so much. It is unfair that her time was tragically cut short but the impact she had during her short life was remarkable. I know she is there watching over us and I will continue to try to make her proud until the day we meet again.

Friends' Memories: Julianne Elouadih[38]

Erin was always an inspiration to me, and she continues to inspire me every day. I am so blessed to be able to say she was my friend. I know in my heart that, even though she isn't here physically, she is still always watching over us. I hope I continue to make her proud.

Many special events have happened since Erin died. Several of her friends have gotten married or engaged; two cousins and five friends have had eight babies, with two more on the way; a few have finished their master's degrees; her cousin Kevin has had two ordinations, first as a transitional deacon and then as a Catholic priest; her grandmother

VoVo and Josh's grandmother Nanny have both died, as well as Abel's brother Sid, two close family friends, Josh's parents' dog Buddy, and Josh and Erin's cat Elainna; Josh adopted two new pets, a dog named Connor and a cat named Sadie; Josh started making hand-carved Rockers Ranch rocking horse creations inspired by Erin; Dad, Josh's mother, Cindy Washbourne, and I retired; many of Erin's friends got new jobs; we've celebrated cousins' wedding anniversaries; one cousin-in-law and a friend became US citizens; and, of course, many birthdays, including Grammy's ninetieth, and holidays have been celebrated. It is hard to celebrate occasions without Erin physically there, even though we know she is there in spirit—in a bigger way than if she were there physically. It's hard for us because we're only unfulfilled humans, and we want to hear her chat and laugh with us.

Not long after Erin died, in Erin's memory, Abel put a single electric Christmas candle in our center upstairs window. It is the window in Erin's closet. Throughout the past five years, in Erin's writings and other readings I've come across, besides hope, light in the darkness seems to be a major theme. When I look over our years together, lighthouses were close to our hearts. I collected ceramic ones; we had wall pictures, books, photos, and calendars of them. Portland Head Light was especially memorable, as we've had many family gatherings there since Erin was little. It was almost the scene of Josh's proposal to her, so he must have realized the special meaning the site had for us. I knew down deep but never fully realized that Erin was our own beacon of light in the darkness. Such an appropriate analogy! She was always our bright and shining light, always looking for the good in others and bringing us laughs and smiles when we felt sad or sick. Her love for people and animals knew no bounds—except for those spiders! She shared all this not just with us but with all her family and friends—actually, with anyone she came in contact with. What a gift Erin was—and still is—to us all.

PART 6

AFTERWORD

Eventually after waiting and holding on to what
little hope I did have, things worked out.
My prayer life began to get stronger and I started
noticing God quietly working in my life.
In fact I noticed he had been working in my life the
whole time but I just wasn't opening my eyes to it.
—Erin Rodriques, late 2010 (twenty years old)

We didn't fully realize how much Erin had impacted others until after she died. Since then, people have come forward to share their personal stories of Erin. Erin, always the great listener, forever had an open ear for people to get things off their chests, never judging them. People knew their secrets were safe with her. They knew someone cared about them. She loved everyone as her best friend. Erin was genuine. She could light up a room with her quiet warmth. When people used to ask me why we homeschooled, I told them, "My goal is to get Erin to Heaven, not Harvard." I'm pretty sure we accomplished that goal because of her loving and caring spirit.

A friend of ours, Deacon Paul Kline, after reading this manuscript, wrote this to us:

> From the time Abel first shared a few of the pages from Erin's diary I was captivated by her unique voice and by the deep wisdom of her words. I think we have fallen into the trap of treating saints and prophets as rare exceptions. Erin's words, to me, reveal the simple but profound truth that each one of us is called to reveal God's love and mercy to others. That is, I think, the meaning of the beautiful prayer whispered into the infant's Spirit at Baptism— "May the Lord open your ears to hear his Word and your mouth to proclaim his glory." Erin's ministry to others (even now!) is testimony to her desire to follow the grace of her baptism as perfectly as she could![39]

Paul Kline's words in the passage above about how we often treat saints and prophets as rare exceptions bring to mind the concept of

New York Times best-selling author and founder of Dynamic Catholic Institute, Matthew Kelly's must-read book entitled *The Biggest Lie in the History of Christianity.* Without divulging what the "biggest lie" is, I want to share just a small part of his book that is relevant to this topic of saints and prophets. In his short but fully packed, challenging book, Kelly explains that, in fact, "[Saint] Paul was abundantly clear in 1 Thessalonians 4:3 that the very will of God is our holiness. God wants us to live holy lives, grow in character and virtue, and become the-best-version-of-ourselves." Kelly continues that holiness is not about being perfect. He reminds us that "these men and women that we place on pedestals would be the first to admit that they did not live holy lives—they lived Holy Moments." Kelly defines a Holy Moment "as a moment when you are being the person God created you to be, and you are doing what you believe God is calling you to do in that moment. It is an instance where you set aside self-interest, personal desire, and what you feel like doing or would rather be doing, and embrace what you believe will bring the most good to the most people in that moment." A Holy Moment is a thing of beauty and can be replicated by you and those who are the recipients of Holy Moments. He suggests that we try to perform a lot of individual Holy Moments, beginning with a single one, such as smiling at a cashier who looks like he's having a bad day. It gives the cashier a Holy Moment in addition to our own. Other simple opportunities include mowing the lawn for a sick neighbor, offering to drive someone who has no transportation, and stopping at a retirement home to visit those who have no visitors. There are many more examples in his book. The opportunities are endless.

As we feel the encouragement from these moments, and if we multiply them each day, the world can become a better and more hopeful place. "Goodness, beauty, and hope—these are things that people need," Kelly writes. He continues, "In a world that can seem so dark at times, God gives you and me a candle and a match and says, 'You are the light of the world,'" and expects us to go out and make a lot of Holy Moments to encourage each other while bringing the goodness, beauty, and hope we all deserve.[40] I believe that Erin lived a life packed with Holy Moments.

At the end of the day, as can be seen in her writings, Erin knew she was never alone. God was her friend. He is there for everyone, as He said. He was always there for her. Jesus told us, "I am with you always, until the end of the age" (Matthew 28:20 NAB). He said, "I *am* with you," not "I *will be* with you." He is here now.

In her silence, as we see in her journals, Erin seemed to have conversations with Him. I strongly believe she heard His comments—and I hope you will too. Please look for those "flickers of light in the deep darkness" that Erin wrote about on December 12, 2005.

The more I study Erin's life through our own memories and through the stories told to us by her friends and family, the more I can see how her life personified—and still does personify—the Peace Prayer of St. Francis. I have added the prayer to the next page so you can see what I mean. It summarizes Erin! She was an instrument of God's peace. She let her light brighten the darkness around her and brought hope to those who had none.

My wish for you in reading this book is for Erin to inspire you in your own lives. Give yourself some quiet time to find your real self. Acknowledge your blessings in thankfulness, and in turn, help people in their times of need. Create your own Holy Moments. Give people five minutes of your time or even a mere smile. You don't know how that seemingly small gesture may make a world of difference in their lives. You might be the "flicker of light" in their darkness while bringing light to your own. Please help light up the world!

The Peace Prayer of St. Francis

Lord, make me an *instrument of your peace.*

Where there is hatred**,** *let me sow love*;

where there is injury, *pardon*;

where there is doubt**,** *faith*;

where there is despair, *hope*;

where there is darkness, *light***;**

where there is sadness, *joy.*

O Divine Master, grant that I may not so much
seek to be consoled as *to console,*

to be understood as *to understand,*

to be loved as *to love.*

For it is in *giving* that we receive,

it is in *pardoning* that we are pardoned,

and it is in dying that we are born to eternal life.

—Anonymous[41] (emphasis mine)

World Youth Day in Cologne, Germany, August 2005. Photo
credit Patrick Logan, used with permission.

Appendix A

RESOURCES

Brodeur, Katie, et al. *Erin Kate Rodriques*. 2014. bookemon.com.

New American Bible. Saint Joseph edition. New York: Catholic Book Publishing Company, 1991.

Rodriques, Kathy. *Erin Child of God*. 2017. picaboo.com.

APPENDIX B

MORE ABOUT ERIN

Website: www.KathyRodriques.com
It can be a place for you to share your personal story of Erin's inspiration.

Facebook: Facebook.com/KathyRodriquesAuthor

Twitter: Twitter.com/KathyRodriques

Email: kathyrodriques@gmail.com

APPENDIX C

INSPIRATIONAL QUOTES

To do many things and to mix with many people, yet not to turn aside from either God or oneself, is a great and rare art.
— St. Ignatius of Loyola (1491–1556)[42]

Be who God meant you to be and you will set the world on fire.
— St. Catherine of Siena (1347–1380)[43]

If you are going through a hard time … please, NEVER lose hope! God is always there for you and He will never leave your side.
— Erin Rodriques, May 26, 2006

Please just place all your worries in His hands and let His Will be done, it will all be good, this I promise you! I will be praying for you.
— Erin Rodriques, May 26, 2006

So, whoever may be reading this, do not worry yourself with things of old or happy moments that have come and gone, but make brand new ones each second of the day. Make every moment very special. Live your life to the very fullest that it can possibly be. I really hope you do.
— Erin Rodriques, July 20, 2005

That is how I try to make my life. Bring out that light. To find that little flicker of light in a world that is full of deep darkness. It is the way I must live.
— Erin Rodriques, December 12, 2005

I love you Lord and I need You. Please be always at my side and help me even when I do not think to ask. I can never thank You enough for all that You have done for me.

—Erin Rodriques, December 20, 2005

If it is His Will, we shall be together someday on this earth and if it is not His Will for us to meet again on this earth than [sic] we shall all definitely meet in the next life and it will be the greatest thing to ever happen.

—Erin Rodriques, May 26, 2006

Quiet prayer for me is what gave me the greatest hope. Speak to God, even if you don't think He's there, don't worry, He's just quietly listening.

—Erin Rodriques, fall 2010

Through this experience I was able to learn to look for God in little ways and notice how His blessings are all around you. Now whenever I reach a dark point in my life, I know to look around me and realize how He is always there.

—Erin Rodriques, late 2010

If you are ever having trouble hoping, look at the small moments that God is quietly putting in your life to show you that He's there and to keep holding on.

—Erin Rodriques, late 2010

Speak tenderly to them. Let there be kindness in your face, your eyes, in your smile, in the warmth of your greeting. Always have a cheerful smile. Don't only give your care, but give your heart as well.

—St. Mother Teresa of Calcutta (1910–1997)[44]

If you judge people, you have no time to love them.

—St. Mother Teresa of Calcutta (1910–1997)[45]

Before you speak, it is necessary for you to listen,
for God speaks in the silence of the heart.
　　　　　　　—St. Mother Teresa of Calcutta (1910–1997)[46]

Let nothing disturb you, Let nothing frighten you, All things
are passing away: God never changes. Patience obtains all
things. Whoever has God lacks nothing; God alone suffices.
　　　　　　　—St. Teresa of Avila (1515–1582)[47]

A word or a smile is often enough to put
fresh life in a despondent soul.
　　　　　　　—St. Thérèse of Lisieux (1873–1897)[48]

Miss no single opportunity of making some small sacrifice,
here by a smiling look, there by a kindly word; always
doing the smallest right and doing it all for love.
　　　　　　　—St. Thérèse of Lisieux (1873–1897)[49]

Sometimes our light goes out, but it is blown again into flame
by an encounter with another human being; each of us owes
deepest thanks to those who have rekindled this inner light.
　　　　　　　—Dr. Albert Schweitzer (1875–1965)[50]

Our souls are not hungry for fame, comfort, wealth, or power.
Those rewards create almost as many problems as they solve. Our
souls are hungry for meaning, for the sense that we have figured
out how to live so that our lives matter, so that the world will be
at least a little bit different for our having passed through it.
　　　　　　　—Rabbi Harold Kushner (1935–)[51]

But at the end, if we are brave enough to love, if we are strong
enough to forgive, if we are generous enough to rejoice in another's
happiness, and if we are wise enough to know that there is enough
love to go around for us all, then we can achieve a fulfillment that
no other living creature will ever know. We can reenter Paradise.
　　　　　　　—Rabbi Harold Kushner (1935–)[52]

In addition to the above quotes, I want to recommend the inspirational movie *All or Nothing*, which is available at https://www.sisterclare.com/en/. This movie details the life of a vibrant young Irish nun who died at the age of thirty-three during an earthquake in Ecuador on April 16, 2016. Her life's messages are similar to Erin's.

Appendix D

Grief and Recovery Resources

Support Groups

Emmaus Ministry for Grieving Parents: https://www.emfgp.org (I am personally familiar with this group.)

Compassionate Friends: https://www.compassionatefriends.org (I have not personally participated in this group.)

Local church or community groups

Books on Grief

Blot, Francois Rene. *In Heaven, We'll Meet Again.* Sophia Institute Press, 2016.

Ketring, Emily. *An Angel of the Beatitudes: Finding Faith after the Loss of a Child.* 2017.

Schwiebert, Pat, and Chuck DeKlyen. *Tear Soup: A Recipe for Healing after Loss.* 6th ed. GriefWatch. 2006.

Spitzer, Robert. *The Light Shines on in the Darkness: Transforming Suffering through Faith.* Vol. 4 of *Happiness, Suffering, and Transcendence.* San Francisco, CA: Ignatius Press, 2017.

APPENDIX E

COMFORTING WORDS

And the ship went out into the High Sea and passed on into
the West, until at last on a night of rain Frodo smelled a sweet
fragrance on the air and heard the sound of singing that came
over the water. And then it seemed to him that as in his dream
in the house of Bombadil, the grey rain-curtain turned all to
silver glass and was rolled back, and he beheld white shores
and beyond them a far green country under a swift sunrise.

—J. R. R. Tolkien (1892–1973)[53]

The soul is not a physical entity, but instead refers to everything
about us that is not physical—our values, memories, identity,
sense of humor. Since the soul represents the parts of the
human being that are not physical, it cannot get sick, it cannot
die, it cannot disappear. In short, the soul is immortal.

—Rabbi Harold Kushner (1935–)[54]

God is the light shining in the midst of darkness, not to deny
that there is darkness in the world but to reassure us that we
do not have to be afraid of the darkness because darkness will
always yield to light. As theologian David Griffin puts it in
God, Power, and Evil, God is all-powerful, His power enables
people to deal with events beyond their control and He gives
us the strength to do those things because He is with us.

—Rabbi Harold Kushner (1935–)[55]

We will meet in heaven. When I go home to God, for
death is nothing else than going home to God, the
bond of love will be unbroken for all eternity.[2]

—St. Mother Teresa of Calcutta (1910−1997)[56]

---

[2] said at the age of eighty while kneeling at the grave of her mother and sister in
Albania (when she was finally allowed to enter Albania) as the sole survivor of
their original family of five

GONE FROM MY SIGHT

I am standing upon the seashore.
A ship at my side spreads her white sails to the morning breeze,
and starts for the blue ocean.

She is an object of beauty and strength,
and I stand and watch her until she hangs like a speck of white cloud
just where the sea and sky come down to mingle with each other.

Then someone at my side says: "There! She's gone!"
Gone where? Gone from my sight—that is all.

She is just as large in mast and hull and spar as she was when she left
my side,
and just as able to bear her load of living freight
to the place of her destination.
Her diminished size is in me, and not in her.

And just at the moment
when someone at my side says: "There! She's gone!"
there are other eyes that are watching for her coming;
and other voices ready to take up the glad shout:
"There she comes!"

—Presumably written by Rev. Luther Beecher (1813–1903) but
has been attributed to Henry Van Dyke (1852–1933) also[57]

DEATH IS NOTHING AT ALL

Death is nothing at all.
It does not count.
I have only slipped away into the next room.
Nothing has happened.

Everything remains exactly as it was.
I am I, and you are you,
and the old life that we lived so fondly together is untouched, unchanged.
Whatever we were to each other, that we are still.

Call me by the old familiar name.
Speak of me in the easy way which you always used.
Put no difference into your tone.
Wear no forced air of solemnity or sorrow.

Laugh as we always laughed at the little jokes we enjoyed together.
Play, smile, think of me, pray for me.
Let my name be ever the household word that it always was.
Let it be spoken without an effort, without the ghost of a shadow upon it.

Life means all that it ever meant.
It is the same as it ever was.
There is absolute and unbroken continuity.
What is this death but a negligible accident?

Why should I be out of mind because I am out of sight?
I am but waiting for you, for an interval,
somewhere very near,
Just round the corner.

All is well.
Nothing is hurt; nothing is lost.
One brief moment and all will be as it was before.
How we shall laugh at the trouble of parting when we meet again!

—Henry Scott Holland (1847–1918)[58]

ONE LAST GLIMPSE

Here is one last glimpse of Erin from her good friend Anna Gorin's point of view. Anna originally posted this on Facebook on December 9, 2015, two years after Erin's death. Anna reposted it on December 9, 2018. Anna and Erin only managed to see each other in person a few times, but they shared many long-distance conversations.

The photo across from this page was taken when Anna was visiting us from Idaho, and she and Erin stopped in at a tea shop in Sandwich, Massachusetts, on Cape Cod.

Anna Gorin **shared a memory.**
December 9 at 4:49 PM ·
I don't think I can say it any better than I have before. Missing you today and all days, Erin, five years later ☐

3 Years Ago

Anna Gorin is with Abel Rodriques and Kathy Rodriques.
December 9, 2015 ·

Some days you will never forget. Two years ago we lost Erin Rodriques to a freak car accident and today those memories of a glimpse into hell that I wouldn't wish on anyone all come flooding back.

The memorials start to look the same after a while, all describing a sweet and kind and nice and quiet girl. Sure, Erin was occasionally those things, but they're far too generic and don't represent someone who was one of my best friends for ten years.

To me Erin was the girl who damaged her vocal cords screaming herself hoarse at a Josh Groban concert, owned a billion pairs of sunglasses, had more crazy drama in her life than anyone else I knew. Preferred the company of animals to most humans, parked at the far end of a parking lot so she wouldn't have to navigate the other cars and called the walking her exercise for the day, worried and analyzed and overthought in the exact same way I did. Developed celebrity obsessions with people no one had ever heard of, called everyone her "best friend" (air quotes included), and had countless people falling in love with her to the point where I'd admonish her for being too nice. Rescued an orphaned baby bird and crafted a nest for it so amazing the rescue organization said it was the best they'd ever seen, used "chickenleg" as a term of endearment for no reason I could ever figure out, loved all things purple, and was never, ever someone I would have called quiet.

I will never forget, I will never stop missing her, and somehow despite today life has to go on.

Photo credit Anna Gorin.

NOTES

Acknowledgments

1   Monsignor John McLaughlin, email message to author, June 27, 2018.
2   Patrick Logan, email message to author, June 27, 2018.
3   Paul Kline, personal letter to author, April 6, 2019.
4   Francesco Cesareo, email to author, November 21, 2018.

Introduction

5   Paul Kline, personal letter to author, April 6, 2019. Includes permission for review on back cover.
6   Carolyn Joyce Carty, reprinted by permission via email to author, March 29, 2019, created 1963, registration number TXu-234-383, February 24, 1986, copyright special codes 1/B///A.

Part 3: Middle Years

7   Joseph Spencer, in *Erin Kate Rodriques*, ed. Katie Brodeur and Friends of Erin (2014), www.bookemon.com.
8   Spencer, *Erin Kate Rodriques*.
9   Erin Rodriques, Facebook timeline, August 16, 2007, album "Josh Groban in Manchester, New Hampshire, 7/27/07."
10 Jon Niven, used with permission given in email message to author, April 26, 2019.

Part 4: Young Adult Years

11 Christian Gobel, email message to author, January 10, 2019.
12 Freymers Beaubrun, email message to author, July 8, 2019.

13 Lauren Milka, in *Erin Kate Rodriques*, ed. Katie Brodeur and Friends of Erin (2014), www.bookemon.com.

14 Caitlin O'Flynn, in *Erin Kate Rodriques*, ed. Katie Brodeur and Friends of Erin (2014), www.bookemon.com.

15 Julianne Elouadih, in *Erin Kate Rodriques*, ed. Katie Brodeur and Friends of Erin (2014), www.bookemon.com.

16 Katie Brodeur, in *Erin Kate Rodriques*, ed. Katie Brodeur and Friends of Erin (2014), www.bookemon.com.

17 Matthew Morrison, used with permission given in email message to author, April 23, 2019.

18 Stephanie Giguere, in *Erin Kate Rodriques*, ed. Katie Brodeur and Friends of Erin (2014), www.bookemon.com.

19 Brodeur, *Erin Kate Rodriques*.

20 Anthony Rofino, in *Erin Kate Rodriques*, ed. Katie Brodeur and Friends of Erin (2014), www.bookemon.com.

Part 5: From Erin's Physical Death to Her New Life

21 Patricia Johnston, email messages to author, September 17, 19, and 21, 2018.

22 Crismel Calderon, used with permission given in email message to author, April 23, 2019.

23 Father Vo Tran Gia Dinh, from *Erin Kate Rodriques Memorial Garden Dedication*, DVD, September 14, 2014.

24 Francesco Cesareo, from *Erin Kate Rodriques Memorial Garden Dedication*, DVD, September 14, 2014.

25 Father Barry Bercier, from *Erin Kate Rodriques Memorial Garden Dedication*, DVD, September 14, 2014.

26 Erin Sullivan, from *Erin Kate Rodriques Memorial Garden Dedication*, DVD, September 14, 2014.

27 Elisabeth Solbakken, from *Erin Kate Rodriques Memorial Garden Dedication*, DVD, September 14, 2014.

28 Lee Pearson, from *Erin Kate Rodriques Memorial Garden Dedication*, DVD, September 14, 2014.

29 Michele Fortin Aubin, from *Erin Kate Rodriques Memorial Garden Dedication*, DVD, September 14, 2014.

30 Arthur Siegel, from *Erin Kate Rodriques Memorial Garden Dedication* DVD, September 14, 2014.

31 Charles "Mike" Land, from *Erin Kate Rodriques Memorial Garden Dedication* DVD, September 14, 2014.

32 Paul Shields, from *Erin Kate Rodriques Memorial Garden Dedication* DVD, September 14, 2014.

33   Anthony Rofino, from *Erin Kate Rodriques Memorial Garden Dedication* DVD, September 14, 2014.

34   Susan Sabelli, from *Erin Kate Rodriques Memorial Garden Dedication* DVD, September 14, 2014.

35   Molly Sweeney, used with permission given in email message to author, April 23, 2019.

36   Paul Kline, personal letter to author, April 6, 2019.

37   Katie Brodeur, in *Erin Kate Rodriques*, ed. Katie Brodeur and Friends of Erin (2014), www.bookemon.com.

38   Julianne Elouadih, in *Erin Kate Rodriques*, ed. Katie Brodeur and Friends of Erin (2014), www.bookemon.com.

Part 6: Afterword

39   Paul Kline, personal letter to author, April 6, 2019.

40   Matthew Kelly, *The Biggest Lie in the History of Christianity* (North Palm Beach, FL: Blue Sparrow Books, 2018), 33, 36, 37, 43.

41   Anonymous, *La Clochette*, December 12, 1912, 285, http://www.franciscan-archive.org/franciscana/peace.html.

Appendix C: Inspirational Quotes

42   St. Ignatius of Loyola, in *Thoughts of St. Ignatius of Loyola for Every Day of the Year*, from the Scintillae Ignatianae compiled by Gabriel Hevenesi, trans. Alan McDougall (New York: Fordham University Press, 2006), 64.

43   Shelley Emling, *Setting the World on Fire* (New York: St. Martin's Press, 2016), xvii. Sourced from *The Letters of Catherine of Siena*, 4 vols., ed. and trans. Suzanne Noffke (Tempe, AZ: Arizona Center for Medieval and Renaissance Studies, 2000, 2001, 2007, 2009), common paraphrase from letter T368.

44   Susan Conroy, *Mother Teresa's Lessons of Love and Secrets of Sanctity* (Huntington, Indiana: Our Sunday Visitor Publishing Division, 2003), 94.

45   "Mother Teresa," accessed April 2, 2019, http://www.famousinspirationalquotes. net/authors/mother-teresa.

46   Mother Teresa, *Essential Writings*, introd. Jean Maalouf (Maryknoll, NY: Orbis Books, 2001), 138.

47   St. Teresa of Avila, "Poem IX," in *Saint Teresa of Jesus: The Complete Works*, trans. and ed. E. Allison Peers, vol. 3 (New York: Sheed and Ward, 1963), common paraphrase 288.

48   St. Thérèse of Lisieux, *The Story of a Soul: The Autobiography of St. Thérèse of Lisieux with Additional Writings and Sayings of St. Thérèse*, ed. Rev. T. N. Taylor, 8th ed. (London: Burnes, Oates, and Washbourne, 1912, 1922).

49 St. Thérèse of Lisieux, *Story of a Soul: The Autobiography of St. Thérèse of Lisieux*, trans. John Clarke, (Washington, DC: ICS Publications, 1996), common paraphrase 196, also accessed April 17, 2019, https://ocarm.org/en/content/ocarm/therese-lisieux-quotes.

50 Conroy, *Mother Teresa's Lessons of Love and Secrets of Sanctity*, 229.

51 Harold S. Kushner, *When All You've Ever Wanted Isn't Enough: The Search for a Life That Matters* (New York: Pocket Books, 1987), 18.

52 Harold S. Kushner, *How Good Do We Have to Be? A New Understanding of Guilt and Forgiveness* (Canada: Little, Brown, and Company Limited, 1996), 181.

Appendix E: Comforting Words

53 J. R. R. Tolkien, *The Return of the King* (New York: Houghton Mifflin, 1994), 1,007. Permission given in email to author, April 10, 2019, from Houghton Mifflin Harcourt.

54 Harold S. Kushner, AZQuotes.com, accessed April 3, 2019, https://www.azquotes.com/quote/871336.

55 Harold S. Kushner, *Overcoming Life's Disappointments* (New York and Canada: Borzoi by Alfred A. Knopf, 2006), 15; ending is a common paraphrase as seen at https://www.goodreads.com/quotes/search?utf8=✓&q=God+is+the+light+shining+in+the+midst+of+darkness%2C+not+to+deny&commit=Search.

56 Eileen Egan and Kathleen Egan, *Suffering into Joy: What Mother Teresa Teaches about True Joy* (Ann Arbor, Michigan: Servant Publications, 1994), 69.

57 At least three publications credit the poem to Rev. Luther Beecher in printings shortly after his death in 1904, but it has also been attributed to Henry Van Dyke, probably due to his name appearing as its author in a widely distributed hospice booklet by Barbara Karnes since 1985. In an email to the author, Barbara Karnes's office stated that it is in the public domain. The following useful websites were accessed March 28, 2019: https://en.wikipedia.org/wiki/Gone_from_my_sight, and http://www.yourdailypoem.com/listpoem.jsp?poem_id=2502.

58 Henry Scott Holland, in a sermon May 1910, accessed April 22, 2019, https://en.wikipedia.org/wiki/Henry_Scott_Holland; also accessed April 22, 2019, https://www.familyfriendpoems.com/poem/death-is-nothing-at-all-by-henry-scott-holland.

BIBLIOGRAPHY

Brodeur, Katie, and Friends of Erin. *Erin Kate Rodriques.* 2014. <u>www.</u>
<u>bookemon.com</u>.

Conroy, Susan. *Mother Teresa's Lessons of Love and Secrets of Sanctity.*
Huntington, Indiana: Our Sunday Visitor Publishing Division,
2003.

Egan, Eileen, and Kathleen Egan. *Suffering into Joy: What Mother Teresa
Teaches about True Joy.* Ann Arbor, Michigan: Servant Publications,
1994.

Emling, Shelley. *Setting the World on Fire.* New York: St. Martin's Press,
2016.

Erin Kate Rodriques Memorial Garden Dedication. DVD. Worcester:
Assumption College, 2014.

Kelly, Matthew. *The Biggest Lie in Christianity.* North Palm Beach, FL:
Blue Sparrow Books/Dynamic Catholic, 2018.

Kushner, Harold S. *How Good Do We Have to Be? A New Understanding
of Guilt and Forgiveness.* Canada: Little, Brown, and Company
Limited, 1996.

Kushner, Harold S. *Overcoming Life's Disappointments.* New York and
Canada: Borzoi by Alfred A. Knopf, 2006.

Kushner, Harold S. Quote retrieved April 20, 2019. https://www.
azquotes.com/quote/871336.

Kushner, Harold S. *When All You've Ever Wanted Isn't Enough: The
Search for a Life That Matters.* New York: Pocket Books, 2015.

"Mother Teresa." Accessed April 2, 2019, <u>http://www.</u>
<u>famousinspirationalquotes.net/authors/mother-teresa</u>.

Mother Teresa. *Essential Writings.* Maryknoll, NY: Orbis Books, 2001.

"Peace Prayer of St Francis." Original source *La Clochette*. 1912. http://www.franciscan-archive.org/franciscana/peace.html.

St. Catherine of Siena. *The Letters of Catherine of Siena*. 4 vols. Edited and translated by Suzanne Noffke. Tempe, AZ: Arizona Center for Medieval and Renaissance Studies, 2009.

St. Ignatius of Loyola. *Thoughts of St. Ignatius of Loyola for Every Day of the Year*. Compiled by Gabriel Hevenesi. Translated by Alan McDougall. New York: Fordham University Press, 2006.

St. Teresa of Avila. "Poem IX." In *Saint Teresa of Jesus: The Complete Works*. Vol. 3. Edited and translated by E. Allison Peers. New York: Sheed and Ward, 1963.

St. Thérèse of Lisieux. *The Story of a Soul: The Autobiography of St. Thérèse of Lisieux*. Translated by John Clarke. Washington, DC: ICS Publications, 1996.

St. Thérèse of Lisieux. *The Story of a Soul: The Autobiography of St. Thérèse of Lisieux with Additional Writings and Sayings of St. Thérèse*. Edited by Rev. T. N. Taylor. 8th ed. London: Burnes, Oates, and Washbourne, 1922. Kindle.

Tolkien, J. R. R. *The Return of the King*. New York: Houghton Mifflin, 1994.

ABOUT THE AUTHOR

Born and raised in the Deering Center area of Portland, Maine, Kathleen Scanlon Rodriques graduated from St. Joseph's Academy there. Her BS degree in pharmacy from Northeastern University in Boston; her work for over forty years in the pharmacy department at McLean Hospital in Belmont, MA; and two bouts of cancer did not prepare her for the tragedy that would befall her family in 2013. Living in Norton, MA for thirty-four years, Kathy has been married to Abel Rodriques since 1981 and they are the proud parents of one daughter, the late Erin Kate Rodriques. Since Erin's unexpected death in 2013, Kathy has been on an emotional roller coaster creating Erin's biography and compiling excerpts from the memorable journals that Erin fortuitously left behind. She is certain that Erin's words need to be shared with this often dark world.